HOW NOT TO RUIN YOUR KIDS

A Practical Guide to Raising Happy, Independent, Equipped Children

Michele Kelber

Mom & Dad, Thank you for being revolutionaries and doing your best as parents even when life threw you curveballs. I think I did you proud.

Gerry & Colette, Thank you for making me a parent and yet still treating me like a daughter and sister. It's our chosen family that often is our beacon.

Table of Contents

CHAPTER 1
Why This Book? 1

CHAPTER 2
Philosophies & Policies 13

CHAPTER 3
Where Kids Are 25

CHAPTER 4
Where We Are as a Society 49

CHAPTER 5
The Importance of Play 67

CHAPTER 6
Responsibility 87

CHAPTER 7
Independence 99

CHAPTER 8
General Life Skills 111

CHAPTER 9
Talking About the Hard Stuff 133

CHAPTER 10
Being of Service 147

CHAPTER 11
Snitches Get Stitches 153

CHAPTER 12
When Is the Right Time? 165

CHAPTER 13
A Note on Parenting 171

CHAPTER 1

Why This Book?

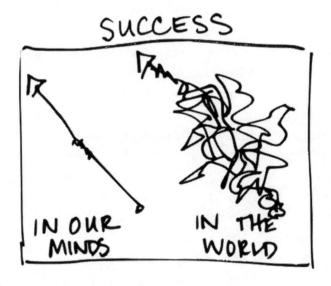

I'm not sure about you, but the image above is a clear, truthful illustration of my success.

But before we get into all that, here's a little about me...

My first higher education adventure was to earn a BA in Fine Arts (sculpture) with a Spanish Minor. After that, I waited tables and considered what to do with my life. Should I get a Master of Fine Arts (MFA) to teach, or a Master of Business Administration (MBA), or go to law school (where I would get a Juris Doctor, or JD)?

I had always thought I'd make a good lawyer and even dreamed about becoming one back in elementary school. I'm not sure what happened in between my 4th-grade debates with my parents about gender equality (I had an older brother) and my college applications that swayed me away from law. Somewhere along my journey, I had let that dream go. But there, at the restaurant, I was rejuvenated whenever I thought of becoming an attorney. Besides, law school had no prerequisites, which might make it harder to get into, but I wouldn't have to catch up on coursework like I would if I chose to go to business school—and those additional classes came at an extra hefty financial cost

So, I applied to law school and got in! It was one of my proudest moments. The whole experience was brag-worthy, as I did it myself and on my own dime. In the end, I earned a dual degree JD/MBA. Since the MBA tuition was wrapped up in my law school tuition, I thought, *Why wouldn't I get an MBA too?* In retrospect, "Why wouldn't I?" was a question I should have answered beforehand. And the answer was "Because that's a lot of work to finish on time!

I spent the winter sessions and summers in class all while also working full time. But I did it. What I hope you take away from my story is that I know how to hustle, I have a solid work ethic, and I possess an entrepreneurial spirit. My childhood summer days were spent selling lemonade, pitching neighbors to mow their lawns, and, of course, selling all the Girl Scout cookies possible each fundraising season.

A Journey of Self-Discovery

I graduated in 2001, moved back to the New York City Metro area, and then the world fell apart. I didn't pass the New York State Bar on the first try and jobs were few and far between after the 9/11 attacks. I worked in disaster recovery and business continuity planning for a few years before I moved back into the legal world. And even then, I ended up in conference rooms turned "offices on document review duty where I was looking for the smoking gun.

I was treated badly by my supervisors and other employees and I didn't easily understand half of what I was reading. Despite that, I stayed the course and ended up defending third-party lawsuits involving companies that no longer existed in the embattled subprime mortgage mess— for years.

If you get a chance, watch the Big Short. Or better yet, skip to the scene where Anthony Bourdain, may he rest in peace, explains everything via a soup metaphor. Just Google "Anthony Bourdain Big Short Soup." It's pure magic.

As you can imagine, my soulless existence in a windowless "office took all the glam and excitement out of the career I had worked so hard to enter. Eleven years after graduating, I got the call saying I was laid off. *Fine by me*, I thought.

My good friends gave me a heartfelt "Congratulations" and "Mazel Tov" when I told them (if you know you know). Next, I spent the summer at my parent's bungalow on Long Beach Island at the Jersey Shore enjoying the freedom of a sun-filled break. It's funny how the universe works, because that September, Super Storm Sandy hit the island, and that was the end of our "Little Piece of Heaven", as Mom coined it. This meant it was time to get serious about my life.

I did a lot of self-discovery work and even dove into the books *Start With Why* and *Find Your Why* by Simon Sinek. If you aren't familiar with his work, Sinek started what he calls a movement, which, at its center, was created to inspire people to live their lives by doing things that inspire them—all while helping them find their "why" to take into the different realms of their professional lives.[1] Both of these books and Sinek's overall philosophy inspired me to go even deeper into my journey of self-discovery and self-awareness.

Honestly, these are great reads to gain insight into what drives you and what may be a great occupational fit for you as well. Once you know the drive behind living your life, everything changes because, at least on some level, many of us have a hard time separating who we are from what we do for work.

These books helped me get out from under the self-imposed expectations I had about what my life was supposed to look like in all its different arenas. See the diagram above. This included work, family, and self.

So many of us just accept the status quo when we really have a thirst for so much more and something so different. The pandemic and lockdowns across the country also shed some light on what we didn't want for ourselves. Mandated work from home in small spaces with partners created spotlights shining on what wasn't working for us anymore. We worked jobs we hated, lived with partners we no longer

---

1   Simon Sinek, "Find Your Why Book: Go beyond Reading," Simon Sinek, accessed August 1, 2023, https://simonsinek.com/books/find-your-why.

loved, and cohabitated in cities and towns that no longer served us. Each one of us might not have known our "why," but we definitely knew our "not why!" Many people made drastic changes and pivoted as only Chandler, Ross, and Rachel could. But did we really come out on the other side with a better understanding of each why for each of our lives? Only you know if you were able to.

I will tell you this, having done the work when it wasn't forced on me, I am crystal clear what my why is. Your why, by the way, is simply your mission statement in life. Your true purpose.

Who I am is a champion of children and women. My why is to help them know their own voices and understand how to use them in pursuit and celebration of a life they love. My why stems from who I am at my core, and that is equity and love. It's why I was called to be a lawyer and why I also left. In the end, my internal compass always pulls me back to equity and love.

So, kids and women? Yep, those are my people. Helping them is who I was in the past and who I am now. I understand the challenges and successes of being both a woman and a child and I want others to be more of who they want to be. It took too long for me to find the keys that enabled me to become the powerhouse that I am, so I want to give you the keys now. That way, you can also hand these keys to your kids.

Again, those years after 4th grade, and then becoming an adult—I was so impressionable. I often ignored my inner compass and then had to fight super hard to get back to it. And now, barely, yes, in my fifti s, I listen to it, I feel it, and I trust it. And I don't give a shit when it doesn't match the expectations of others.

The Future My Keys Unlocked

Let's get back into my success map. After so many years of resisting working with children—I was still getting over the decades of babysitting I had done since I was 11 years old—I was almost finished denying my roots as the child of one educator and one child psychologist. Part of my exploration was asking those closest to me what they saw for me as far as a fitting career

Most pointed to my work with children and my gift of relating to them and championing them. After working with a not-for-pro t that provided tness classes to at-risk youth, I went out on my own and started a few kids' programs in the area. The purpose, which I later realized was *my* purpose, was to provide opportunities for young people to learn life skills and exercise their voice, no matter their ages.

Fitness was just the vehicle we used to deliver those opportunities. It was a way to provide time for free play, practice meaningful risky behavior, and interact with group dynamics in a controlled and safe environment. The program stuck in Long Island City Queens, and the rest, as they say, is history (or HERstory in this case).

A Dream Becomes Reality

The gym I founded—Gantry Kids & Teens—is a manifestation of my mission and also has its own purpose centered on "Building Tomorrow's Leaders Today." Through fitness and movement, kids acquire skills, like learning to be more understanding, which allow them to grow to be successful, self-aware, responsible, and independent individuals.

I've been called a revolutionary, but really, I'm just giving kids a chance. With every rope swing, fort build, box jump, and obstacle overcome, kids learn to problem solve, take risks, use up their energy, cooperate with others, resolve disagreements, lead groups, speak their minds, be responsible, and choose to self-regulate. These are all great qualities for a person to learn if they want to manage their piece of the great big world out there well.

What Are We Preparing Them For?

We try so hard to protect the children in our lives and set them on the right path that we sometimes forget to let them learn, fail, and grow on their own terms. When we do this, we are denying them the tools they need to be independent. Yet, we then expect them to be awesome on their own when they reach a certain age.

Would you expect someone to be able to drive a car if they had never had a driving lesson? So, why do we expect children to become confident, capable young people and adults when we didn't provide them with the related lessons they need to do so? Kids are like blank canvases. We owe them the proper tools to be able to turn those canvases into brilliant works of art—the authentic, unique masterpieces they can become.

Does Your Child Have Access to the Keys They Need?

Circling back, let's think about your unique why. Let's consider your why as it relates to your child. What do you want for them? Many times, we don't think in terms of specific jobs we want for them or specific amounts of money in their bank accounts we hope they'll achieve. Instead, we think about how we want our children to be happy, experience love, be successful, and have the strength to handle the bumpy parts of life.

If you are interested in those things, keep reading. This book is a culmination of my life's work of advocating for children. "Building Tomorrow's Leaders Today" is an expression of how we encourage children to know their own voices and to use them in pursuit and celebration of lives they love. It is my goal to present opportunities for kids to learn necessary life skills which will lead them to be successful, act even when they are unsure or anxious, shoot for the moon, learn from failure and get back up when they fail, take care of business, support others, and excel despite everything that is in their way.

In the 10+ years that Gantry Kids & Teens has been around, and in my 30+ combined years of mentoring, coaching, fostering, and championing children, I have seen a lot. This book is my gift to the world, with help that goes beyond the walls of the gym, to share what I've seen that has worked for kids along with what has made tremendous differences in their lives and the lives of their families. Before we move on, I need you to consider one thing: What is your "why" when it comes to your children?

We're going to walk through thinking about this "why" in the next few paragraphs, but you can also grab the worksheet for determining your "why" for your children in our reader resources.

If you aren't sure, or are having a hard time articulating what it is you want for each child, take a few minutes. Close your eyes and just see what visuals come to mind. Your child is smiling, running, playing freely, sharing with others, showing empathy and grace to someone in need, reaching milestones in life, and achieving great things. Think about how that makes you feel. Happy, proud, illuminated. Look at the emotions on their face.

Go for the big picture rather than specifics. You are committed to their happiness and well-being, but how all that plays out is really up to them. I'd say that for most of us, our why for the children in our lives is for them to be happy, loving, and successful. So, grab onto that, and be open to what their joy looks like. It might be different than what you originally thought!

Also, don't be afraid to ask *them* what *they* want. As adults, people often search back to the things that they liked doing as a child to determine what their own children should be doing right now. A child's aspirations are the purest form of their why. John Lennon once explained that his teacher had asked him what he wanted to be when he grew up. His response was that he wanted to be happy. She told him he didn't get the point of the assignment to which he responded that she must not get the point of life.[2]

My point is, our desires and wishes for each child in our lives is rooted in ethos and love, not a specific career or a certain amount of money in their bank account. What we want at our core is for them all to be happy, loving, and independent humans.

For many families, this book will be an amazing resource as it guides them through the different methods and systems that will help them equip their child to live

---

2   Martin O'Gorman and Radio X, "The Truth behind John Lennon's 'Happy' Quote," Radio X, October 9, 2020, https://www.radiox.co.uk/artists/john-lennon/truth-behind-john-lennon-happy-quote.

a happy, fulfilled, and high-functioning life. For others, it will serve as a starting point.

Because it is my goal to help as much as I can when help is needed, I have created group coaching that will allow you to go through each of the lessons I'm giving in this book, with so much more, alongside other parents and guardians who are trying their best to give their kids joy-filled lives. I'll mention it again at the end of the book.

A note to people who work with kids: I already know that in many ways, the kids you work with feel like *your* kids. That's how much you care. If you're reading this book because you're a worker or director of a children's program and know you can do better, awesome. You're in the perfect place. In fact, I even do consulting for organizations like yours if you want to follow up with hands-on support after you finish the book, or as you are reading it! There will be more details about this in the final chapter for those looking for extra guidance.

This book will help guide you along your parenting journey, whatever your family looks like, to support the children around you to experience independent growth and development toward a life that they too love. So, go get your second cup of co ee, hunker down, and read on, my friends. Read on.

There's one last thing to go over before we really get into the life-changing strategies that are going to totally transform your parenting. It is my goal to support you in the best way I can. That's why I have different ways for us to interact. If you'd like to join my email newsletter, I'll send you important tips and information as you go on this self-awareness and kid-awareness journey. And in exchange for your email (because I know you don't give it out to just anyone), I'll send you a copy of my one-of-a-kind resource that teaches you and your children how to have better conversations with each other. Are you in?

Reader Resources

Head to
https://hownottoruinyourkids.com/reader-extras
to get signed up today.

CHAPTER 2

Philosophies & Policies

I get so many compliments on how the gym is run and the philosophy behind it. Parents think I'm some kind of revolutionary, but I'm not. Like most people these days, I'm stating and executing something in a way that is palatable and enticing to people. They are drawn to it. Some parents send their kids to our programs simply because they want us to do the heavy lifting.

They know it provides so much for their child, and it's *easier* to have us execute than for them to do it themselves—at least in the beginning. Attempting to create independent, autonomous kids can feel scary! I take the liability, encourage the risk-taking, and the payoff is priceless. I'm used to seeing kids swing on ropes 15 feet off the ground—their guardians don't need the risk-related heart attack!

We are super clear about our philosophies and strict about our policies at the gym. Why? Too many businesses are strong-armed or swayed by what their customers want, and therefore are not driven by what people actually need.

We do internal check-ins often about our practices to determine if the exceptions and compassion we show to our parents are actually serving them and us. See, our philosophies are our promises to you to deliver a great program: and our policies are our word in the world so that everyone knows what to expect. Faltering on either can create an unclear, chaotic mess, and who wants that? Brené Brown puts it simply when she states in one of her keynote speeches that clarity is kindness. It really is. The clearer you can be with someone, the kinder it is for everyone because people are aware of what's expected. With clarity involved, there is no guesswork in the relationship. This eff rt creates a great solid foundation for relationships based on mutual respect.

Our philosophy can be found on our website gantrykids.com, but for reference and ease:

Gantry Kids & Teens is about creating opportunities for kids to learn important life skills. They can be flexing muscles in leadership, risk taking, courage, managing expectations, experiencing nervousness, being a part of a team, communicating what you need, and even being a friend. All of our programs, especially our Camps, and After School allow our athletes to play freely without adult intervention. It's in these moments that children learn the skills needed to become well adjusted, empathetic, and successful adults.

Fitness is our platform. Coach-directed classes and play are also essential in our philosophy. Box jumps, rope swings, and hanging upside down on the rings are just a few ways to initiate growth, individually and as a team. When a child succeeds at the task at hand, whether with a little coaching or on their own, they have the magical ability to let it transform their entire lives. They leave the gym with a skip in their step ready to take on the world! If only adults did the same. The added bonus of being physically fit makes Gantry Kids & Teens a winning equation!

And then there are the teens! Although our Pre-Teens and Teens Classes are structured a bit differently, the philosophy stays the same. We are committed to the personal autonomy of each of our athletes. We are each responsible for the choices we make, whether it's showing up on time, effectively strategizing a workout, giving ourselves a pass when it gets too hard, or PRing a lift, we live with the results. Our aim is to give our teens a taste of what's possible and have them choose for themselves which path to take, showing them that hard work pays off and sometimes being a little uncomfortable is worth the pot of gold at the end.

No matter what age your child is, or what program your child participates in, they will get the best of us in any moment. Gantry Kids & Teens is about empowering young people to face the world! We are literally "Building Tomorrow's Leaders Today." We hope you are too!

How and why did I come up with this? A ton came from my own experience working with kids. I have always been in the arena, starting when I was merely 11 years old, babysitting a seven-month-old boy. You read that right: an 11-year-old in charge of an *infant*.

I was mature for my age, it was the '80s, and my parents were always either around the corner or a phone call away. I continued babysitting for that family, and in fact, am still incredibly close with them. I helped with all four kids, who are now grown, getting married, and having their own babies. Good grief, I'm old! How did that happen?

Truthfully, in a way, they helped raise me too. In fact, at one of their weddings during open mic at the rehearsal dinner, I was prodded to share my pearls of wisdom, so I obliged. Misty-eyed, I directed my attention to his betrothed and wished her the joy of being a part of the family meaning she too would receive the endless love and nurturing that comes with being a member of their tribe. I told them my hope was that she could grow up while they grow old together, just like I had the pleasure of doing over all these years. It still moves me to think about that moment and every one in between as the relationships with all four kids had me go from acting in a parental role to me being a friend. We'll talk more about that later in the book, too.

Don't worry, I also shared the indiscretions and questionable choices I made navigating secrets and coverups along the way. Again, we *all* grew up together. Anyway, besides being a sort of teen mom, I also worked at various summer camps over the years, was a mentor at various large organizations for children, led a not-for-profit for at-risk youth as the executive director, and even went on to be a licensed foster parent for a while. Something I would love to do again.

I have learned so much about kids and raising great humans by being in the arena and doing the work hands on. I've attended countless workshops and trainings to be a better mentor and foster parent, especially to children who come from challenging social and economic backgrounds, where maybe the adults in their lives were doing their best, but still came up short.

Now, to add to my life-long learning approach, I read countless books, listen to podcasts, and source various philosophies from social media outlets. I also pull from my own experiences growing up in the '70s and '80s, in what would now be termed a free-range childhood, being raised by mostly hands-off parents. We just called it living and it was glorious!

The philosophy of the gym is based on what seems to be common sense to me and has been shown to work best. There are definite similarities between the Montessori Method, Sudbury Model, and various self-directed learning methods. While reading about these approaches has been helpful, the biggest gift and teacher for me has been being in the actual arena.

Brené[3], yes, we are on a first-name basis (at least in my heart), enlightened me to the arena. Some may call it the trenches (or the weeds if you ever waited tables), but the arena applies a willingness and commitment, rather than subjugation, to something. Brené borrowed this concept from President Teddy Roosevelt's speech, "Citizenship in a Republic":

> "It is not the critic who counts; not the WOman who points out how the strong WOman stumbles or where the doer of deeds could have done them better. The credit belongs to the WOman who is actually in the arena, whose face is marred by dust and sweat and blood; who strives valiantly; who errs, who comes short again and again, because there is no effort without error and shortcoming; but who does actually strive to do the deeds; who knows the great enthusiasms, the

---

3   Bréne Brown, obviously.

great devotions; who spends himself or HERself in a worthy cause; who, at the best, knows, in the end, the triumph of high achievement, and who, at the worst, if She fails, at least She fails while daring greatly, so that HER place shall never be with those cold and timid souls who neither know victory nor defeat."

—Theodore Roosevelt
"Citizenship in a Republic" was given at the Sorbonne in Paris on April 23, 1910

Poetic license was taken above, of course. Representation matters, bitches!

Is This a Good Fit for Our Family?

Simply put, if you aren't 100% aligned with our philosophies, the Gantry Kids' method probably isn't for you. We let kids climb up the rig in the gym and hang out 15 feet above the ground. They climb the ropes, swing across chasms, and jump off boxes ten feet high. We bike all over Queens and Brooklyn during our camps and let the older kids lead the line—in our giant and glorious city! If a coach needs a coffee or is missing a supply for an activity, the elder kids go run the errand, crossing the main street and hitting the deli around the corner.

Kids also clean up their own messes and get delegated other tasks and chores at the gym. It gives them purpose and an understanding that they matter in the world, are a part of this community, and play an important role in both. For some people this is just too much. So, if any part of you wants to opt your child out of what we do, we stand firm and let you know that changing our approach is not possible if you choose to work with us.

We will, however, take the time to explain the risk versus the reward and why we insist on executing this way. The conversation includes, "There needs to be trust between us, and you need to make the right choice for your family. It's okay if Gantry Kids might not be a fit." Most parents trust the process and register their children. Some are too anxious, they don't enroll, and I say a little prayer to the universe that their family finds what they truly need elsewhere, which again, might not be what they think they need or want.

One time, a mom was super upset because a weight had fallen and almost landed on her child's foot. Now, this happened because the little girl was touching the weights and spinning them on their post, something that is against the rules of the gym. Why is it against the rules? Because spinning them makes them come off the post onto nearby feet! The mom questioned me and blamed what she said was our lack of supervision. She wanted to know how I could have let that happen. First, nothing actually happened. Second, her child almost had an accident caused by their own actions.

After validating her feelings, I calmly told her, "Your child is aware of the rules and she was doing something that she knew she wasn't supposed to be doing. Our supervision ratios are more than what is required by law *and* there are expectations for each child to do their part to stay safe. It is not the job of any adult to shield your child from making mistakes and getting hurt." Now, had the child gotten hurt, I still would have held fast, because accidents happen and, in all honesty, she would have ended up with a black toenail at best. It's like Taylor Swift says, this mom needed to calm down.

As the business has grown and I've hired a program manager, I can now take the time to further educate myself, the staff, and even parents on the hows of "building tomorrow's leaders today." A big piece of that is equipping both children and adults with necessary tools in the process. Cough, cough—like this book and other available training! After all, the more independent our kids are the more our lives become too! It's a win-win.

Commitment Matters

Now, what if your community is so hive-minded that your openness to parenting is viewed as neglectful or reckless? In that case, it's time to expand your community and be the shining light on what's important for kids' development. Every person's perspective has the potential to bring something new to the table and it's important to look past the confines of your community to see what is going on in it—especially when it comes to raising children. That's why you're here after all, right? It is my hope that this book provides you with an anchor and a point of view to share with others. Check out the downloadable PDF that has some of my favorite resources, books, podcasts, socials etc. by accessing the reader resources.

Reader Resources

One of the biggest differences between our gym and other child-centered programs is that we don't give refunds. Period. The end. Okay, maybe there's room for a comma since we aren't monsters. But you'll get a credit, not a refund. Why? Well, because you made a commitment.

We provide ample opportunities before any money changes hands to see if your child is a good fit for our program and vice versa. Signing up sight unseen and then not reading our policies and quitting because your child "doesn't like it" is a *you* problem, not a Gantry Kids' problem.

Again, it is important to have conversations about the why that lives behind your kid saying they don't like something. Encourage them to give it another try and use some new strategies to get past whatever it is that is causing the related upset or discomfort. You'll see in the next few chapters, conflict and uncomfortableness are where all the magic happens in child development.

Don't rob your child of the experience of coming out of something on the other side a happy, accomplished, and self-confident young person simply because they are mildly uncomfortable in the moment. The whole "no refunds" concept is so you understand that we all made a commitment and we need to keep our word and see it through.

In our business model, the same applies for missed classes or camps. We don't give make ups. This also has to do with time and money expended with the expectation that a child is going to attend. Shifting them to another day or time just doubles that expenditure. In order to help your community, it's important to stop asking small business to bend to your needs. This is why we have set up our policies to protect our business both in viability and integrity. But there are also important lessons to learn about how to parent your child that are built into these policies.

In other instances, parents have told me they conferred with their child about our policies. That was a huge red flag. In doing so, the grown up had just told their child that the child runs my business and gets to call the shots. If that's how it works in their home, good for them, but that is not how we work at Gantry Kids, or in life for that matter.

Asking any small business to sway from their policies and philosophies is asking them to side step their own integrity. If you don't have your integrity, you don't have much. When you throw this to the wayside, your why and your mission both get diluted. This is why we take a hard stance on making exceptions to the policies in our business, because we don't want to be like the shitty program offerings that are already out there.

Oh, and I have one last note about communication when it comes to sharing successfully with kids who are learning to take risks and be uncomfortable: Stop using adult concepts and words to describe childhood behavior. I bet you that there is a 99% chance that your child was *not* assaulted or bullied in a 1-day camp. Based on the definitions of those words, I can say that with complete confidence—more to come on that later.

When you're looking for the right program or method to help your child, look at the organization's philosophies and see if you are aligned with them. It's a great way to set your expectations and then check in to make sure you are getting what was promised. For programs, look at a company's policies and make sure you can abide by them without asking for special exceptions. These rules are to ensure that a quality program is being offered, expectations are met, and kids are happy and healthy.

And if you're looking for a new method that will help you *not* ruin your kids, now you know why we have these policies and choose to have our team be the ones who adapt the ideas that we use. Do our methods feel like a good fit for where you want your child to end up? Then let's do this.

CHAPTER 3

Where Kids Are

It's important to understand how children grow and develop so that we can support them in positive and useful ways. After all, we want to set up our kids to be outstanding adults. With that in mind, it's best to understand how kids function so we understand how to teach them well. This chapter will discuss cognitive development, psychosocial development, and a tidbit on personalities. It's essential to understand each framework. I'm going to describe it and how it functions so you have the tools you need to elevate your child's growth.

Children learn at different stages and rates. Their cognitive development is dependent upon going through each unique stage. If one is skipped or missed, children are left with deficiencies. In families where children are truly neglected, that cognition never develops and kids end up stuck, functioning at a lower level of learning and comprehension.

I've seen these deficiencies in extreme cases as a foster parent and I've seen them in more nuanced forms as one of the impacts of the pandemic. Kids are behind developmentally because of the lack of social interaction that resulted from social distancing. Now, before you get your boxers in a bunch, this book is not a statement on the legitimacy of COVID 19. This book will speak to the impact we are seeing from the social deficiencies related to social distancing and what we can do about them now.

If you didn't already know, this amazing guy named Jean Piaget was a Swiss psychologist who studied child development and created the Theory of Cognitive Development. His work gained traction in the field in the '60s. Today, Piaget is one of the most cited psychologists of the 20th century.[4] If you're curious, just turn to your favorite search engine to find out more. Piaget believed there were four stages of cognitive development. I'm going to give you a more concise version of those stages here so that they're easier to digest and understand.

---

4   Kendra Cherry, MSEd, "Jean Piaget Biography (1896–1980)," fact checker Emily Swaim, Jean Piaget: Life and Theory of Cognitive Development, November 2, 2022, https://www.verywellmind.com/jean-piaget-biography-1896-1980-2795549#citation-11.

The Four Stages of Cognitive Development
(How Kids Generally Grow & Change Over Time)

STAGE	AGE RANGE	WHAT HAPPENS AT THIS STAGE?
Learning An Outside World Exists	0-2 years old	Infants and toddlers are curious about the outside world and learn about it using their senses. They also start to use verbal cues, including noises and words, along with motions such as pointing to start storing outside information in their minds. They learn that just because they can't see an object, that doesn't mean it ceases to exist.
Observation Turns Into Imagination	2-7 years old	As language develops, they start to use it to express different ideas. At the same time, memory becomes more active. While they are learning how to imagine and also follow the intuition they feel, abstract concepts are still difficult. They start to think about how to keep things the same as they realize there is a past and there will be a future.
Connecting Thoughts to Objects and Events	7-11 years old	They realize that the ideas they have been taught and observed can be directly connected to real-life situations. Concepts of time, space, and quantity become real and can be used as they navigate life, but they aren't able to separate all of those concepts just yet. They also start to think about others more as opposed to focusing on themselves.
Expanded Thinking	11 years old and older	Preteens are starting to have more complicated thoughts that span outside of their general observations. They are thinking about theory, hypothetical situations, and "what if" questions that pull them into thinking that goes against the facts they see and experience. They are also getting better at understanding abstract concepts and logical reasoning. Now, they are able to make plans and use strategy. Plus, they can put different concepts together to see how they work alongside each other. They're also starting to think about society and how they fit into it.

I know this table might feel a bit intimidating at first, so let's break it down. Children are continual sponges; but unlike sponges, they absorb and process differently as they grow. They know nothing when they are born. In modern Greek, the word for baby comes from the word for stupid, meaning that when babies enter the world, they know nothing. I thought that was an interesting way to approaching naming new additions to the human race.

We must teach children everything, including kindness and love. They learn in different ways at different stages. Piaget's Child Development chart, which I've summarized in my own words, breaks down the stages of development. Keep in mind that this is a general guideline. There are a lot of children that can be ahead or behind these specific stages of development.

Again, the pandemic has caused a 2-year delay in many children's development. A 7-year-old child may actually be at the development stage of a 5-year-old. We saw this a lot at Summer Camp in 2022. There were 6-, 7-, and even 8-year-old kids who had no emotional awareness or self-regulation of their emotions. They were experiencing meltdowns customary to toddlers rather than reactions appropriate to their ages. With this in mind, it is vital to remember to be a little patient with your littles.

All the Feels and Some of the Memories

In the early years of life, learning is sensory. That's why I referred to this stage as kids learning an outside world exists. Children aged 1 day to 2 years touch, feel, and look. You can see the evidence of this when babies are always putting things in their mouths. It's a way for them to process and learn. They also start to understand that things still exist even when they can't see them. Peek-a-boo is a fun hilarious game at that age because children are just understanding permanence and that you will come back. And what appears to be separation anxiety may just be a child learning that mama and dada are indeed in the other room for just a moment!

As kids enter the next stage, where observation turns into imagination—ages 2-7, spanning from toddler into school age—they develop memory and understand a little bit about both the past and the future. They know they have a mommy, but when an adult tells a child they too have a mommy, the child may look at them bewildered. "Wait you have a mommy too? But you are a mommy!" They are quickly learning that right now isn't the only time. They may even grow a tiny bit more patient when asked to wait for things because they know there is a future.

This stage, and the remainder of the subsequent stages, span quite a few diverse development check points. Each year, a child has the potential for exponential growth, so even though many ages are categorized in the same stage, their development is wildly varied and will look vastly different for each unique person. Humans are complex, and that's part of the fun of being one and raising others.

During the stage where they connect thoughts and objects to events, ages 7-11, children are just starting to move away from egocentric thinking. That means, for the most part, they are still seeing the world as it relates only to them. Like the cable company, and a lot of men I've dated, children literally think they are the sun and the world revolves around them. The rest of us are just here living in their world.

At this stage, they are beginning to grasp the concept that other people actually exist for an independent purpose that is unrelated to them. However, they do not necessarily transfer knowledge that they understand about themselves to others. So, what hurts or upsets them may not be linked to something that would hurt or upset another person.

For instance, when kids will give you the business, and you give it back, like gentle teasing or poopy-face talk, the tears start flowing—oh do they start to flow. Children feel the impact, but don't necessarily recognize when they are the cause of it. They don't have the ability to realize that under the same circumstances someone else would feel the same. They begin to process the world around them and begin to recognize that they have a place amongst it.

One mistake that I see a lot of well-meaning parents, guardians, and those working with children make is to treat our elementary-school-age children like they are in the expanded thinking stage, which is defined as being ages 11 and up. In this stage, children understand abstract concepts and can apply learned experiences to new situations. They now transfer knowledge.

But before age 11, these ideas are way too advanced for a child that is 7-9 years of age and still in the connecting thoughts to objects and events stage. Expecting a mindset that is on a different developmental level can displace children and stop them from understanding the concepts you are trying to teach. In fact, trying to address them as if they are in the expanded thinking stage when they're not can cause them to question their capabilities as a human. Let's look at an example of how this happens.

As a new chef, would you feel good about yourself if the restaurant you worked in only served Baked Alaska and Beef Wellington? Those are very advanced and difficul meals to make. Of course, you would feel like crap and probably quit your job. You can't throw tantrums and quit because of anger in everyday life, so be aware of meeting your children where they are cognitively and helping them to advance. By helping, I mean making sure there are opportunities for growth. Trying to force progress by guiding them too heavily will only hurt their development, not help it. Check in with yourself if you are often disappointed in the lack of certain behaviors and wondering why these behaviors are inconsistent. It's not always related to willful disobedience from your child and instead could indicate you are expecting them to live in a stage of development they haven't reached yet.

Next Stop, Psychosocial Development

In addition to Piaget's cognitive development, there is also psychosocial development to consider. Erik Erikson was a psychoanalyst and professor. In his book, *Childhood and Society*, Erikson mapped the personal development of humans throughout their lifetimes.[5]

Erikson's eight stages of psychosocial development is psychology's most influential and accepted theory of human development, which replaced Freud's psychosexual schematic. Each of Erikson's stages takes into account biological, psychological, and social factors. The stages span from birth to old age. In each stage, Erikson says there is

---

5   Jeremy Sutton, "Erik Erikson's Stages of Psychosocial Development Explained," PositivePsychology.com, March 9, 2023, https://positivepsychology.com/erikson-stages/.

a natural conflict you will face, and it changes as you get older. If you're curious, do some research to see where you are in your journey according to Erikson and maybe what some of your challenges are based on how you faired in each stage. Here is a breakdown of what the phases look like, in my own words.

What Our Social Development Looks Like According to Age

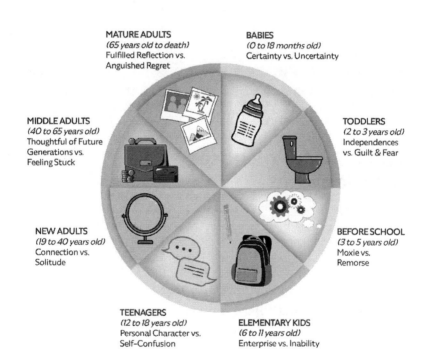

MATURE ADULTS
(65 years old to death)
Fulfilled Reflection vs. Anguished Regret

BABIES
(0 to 18 months old)
Certainty vs. Uncertainty

MIDDLE ADULTS
(40 to 65 years old)
Thoughtful of Future Generations vs. Feeling Stuck

TODDLERS
(2 to 3 years old)
Independences vs. Guilt & Fear

NEW ADULTS
(19 to 40 years old)
Connection vs. Solitude

BEFORE SCHOOL
(3 to 5 years old)
Moxie vs. Remorse

TEENAGERS
(12 to 18 years old)
Personal Character vs. Self-Confusion

ELEMENTARY KIDS
(6 to 11 years old)
Enterprise vs. Inability

What Our Social Development Looks Like According to Age

Babies (0 to 18 months old)
General Conflict: Certainty vs. Uncertainty
Essential Acts: Eating, Feeling Support
Questions They Have: Am I safe where I exist?
What Happens: Tiny humans learn how to feel safe when the people who care for them show up consistently with love and devotion.

Toddlers (2 to 3 years old)
General Conflict: Independences vs. Guilt & Fear
Essential Acts: Learning to use the toilet, Getting Dressed
Questions They Have: Can I only do things if others help me or can I act on my own?
What Happens: As kids grow, they are able to control their movements to gain a sense of autonomy, which is backed up by any successes they have. When they fail, they feel guilt and fear.

Before School (3 to 5 years old)
General Conflict: Moxie vs. Remorse
Essential Acts: Act on Curiosity, Engage in Fun (Freeplay!)
Questions They Have: Am I nice or mean?
What Happens: Kids learn they can affect the world around them and use this power. At this point, when they succeed, they feel purpose. Those who try to use power too much deal with criticism, which makes them feel remorse.

Elementary Kids (6 to 11 years old)

General Conflict: Enterprise vs. Inability
Essential Acts: Going to School
Questions They Have: How can I overcome?
What Happens: Kids are experiencing new social and learning demands, including conflict. When they succeed, they feel better able to take on the next challenge. When they fail, they feel like they can't do anything right.

Teenagers (12 to 18 years old)

General Conflict: Personal Character vs. Self-Confusion
Essential Acts: Building Relationships with Others, Building Identity
Questions They Have: Where am I going and who will I become?
What Happens: They start to feel and build their autonomy and identity. When they succeed, they feel more able to embrace their identities. When they fail, they feel confused about their role in life and that weakens who they feel they are.

New Adults (19 to 40 years old)

General Conflict: Connection vs. Solitude
Essential Acts: Building Close Relationships
Questions They Have: Do people love me? Do they want me around?
What Happens: As they build strong, personal, loving relationships with others, they find that success can create positive, dynamic connections while failure ends up with them feeling or being alone.

Middle Adults (40 to 65 years old)

General Conflict: Thoughtful of Future Generations vs. Feeling Stuck

Essential Acts: Building a career and a family

Questions They Have: Am I creating real value through the way I live?

What Happens: They look to create relationships and projects that will outlast their life spans by having kids or creating change that helps others. When they succeed, they feel valued and accomplished. When they fail, they feel like passive observers in the world.

Mature Adults (65 years old to death)

General Conflict: Fulfilled Reflection vs. Anguished Regret

Essential Acts: Taking an account of life so far

Questions They Have: Have I lived the way I wanted and do I have all I need?

What Happens: They need to process the things that have happened in life so far to feel accomplished in all aspects of living. When they succeed, this makes them feel knowledgeable and experienced. When they fail, they feel remorse and hopelessness.

An important note: Joan Erikson, Erikson's wife added a ninth stage. This stage considers other experiences of continued aging included parts of the eight stages. Joan should be given her due in addition to Erik, as she was a major contributor and partner in developing the work. They were married for 64 years.[6]

Speaking of stages, despite feeling 15, I'm in middle adults right now. Although single and willfully childless, I have fulfilled this stage because my life's work at the gym, mentoring, and writing this book is helping me to create lasting change that will help other people.

I will tell you that as a younger woman working in that windowless offic being treated badly, I did not experience the feeling of achievement related to having successful accomplishments. And while I never felt the pull to be a mother, I definitely have the innate ability to mother, and founding and growing a business is nurturing and providing something for someone other than myself. So, there isn't a one-way road to success when it comes to psychosocial development.

If you look at the stages that covers ages 3 to 18, you'll see that managing conflicts has a tremendous impact on who that child becomes and how they feel about themselves. How many of us avoid conflict for ourselves and on behalf of our children? Too many! Kids today aren't arriving at the necessary outcomes at each stage of development because we manage too much of their lives. We try to

---

6   Gabriel A. Orenstein and Lindsay Lewis, "Eriksons Stages of Psychosocial Development – StatPearls – NCBI Bookshelf," Eriksons Stages of Psychosocial Development, November 7, 2022, https://www.ncbi.nlm.nih.gov/books/NBK556096/.

help them avoid conflict because we don't want them to feel uncomfortable. But, **all the magic happens when we are uncomfortable.** School-age children, if successful in the enterprise versus inability stage, exit that specifi milestone with a feeling of capability.

The key is for their success to be self-driven through their own ability to cope with demands. We can't do it for them, because then it's not truly a success and the child will have no relationship to the achievement. It will be a failure, that leaves them feeling inferior. For instance, let's say your 8-year-old child signed up for a new activity—cooking! After a few sessions, they tell you they don't like it and don't want to go anymore. The key question to be answered according to the stage is "How can I overcome?" They say the way to get to Carnegie Hall is to practice, practice, practice. So, how will quitting make them good? It won't. It eliminates the question, avoids the conflict of enterprise versus inability, and initiates a failure that results in feelings of inferiority.

Sure, your child might play it off or seem not to give a shit, but allowing the impulse to avoid failure to be acted on and repeated will leave your child feeling incompetent long into the future. Will your kid complain and exaggerate and try and manipulate you into changing your mind? Yes! But, it's your job to discuss the importance of following through on commitments and doing a deep dive into what the issue is with the class. You may find out that they made a mistake once and kids laughed, or that the person helping with cooking is being watched by everyone and they are nervous. These are all conflicts that you can talk your child through as you empower them to go outside their comfort zone. This includes showing up after things are hard for them or don't go their way. As hard as it is to persevere in difficul circumstances, avoiding the aftermath of upset can have the same impact as the actual event. Sidestepping issues until things blow over can leave your child feeling disempowered and like a failure. Your goal is to **get them in the arena.**

It's Time to Talk Personalities

While working with so many children over the years, I noticed that there always seem to be at least one or two that don't listen—ever. They argue for arguing's sake. On the flip side, there are those who always do what they are told or manage their business without any adult intervention. So, what creates that big difference in behavior

At their core, it is their identity that drives the behavior, not individual choices per se. When I was doing retrospective work on myself, I participated in an experiment based on *The Happiness Project: Or Why I Spent a Year Trying to Sing in the Morning, Clean My Closets, Fight Right, Read Aristotle, and Generally Have More Fun*, an amazing book by Gretchen Rubin. I strongly recommend reading that book as well as Rubin's other book, *Outer Order Inner Calm: Declutter & Organize to Make More Room for Happiness*. That one is gold because clutter creates an upsetting environment.

Anyhow, Gretchen incorporates building habits as a tenet of how to make changes in your life. She also recommends understanding your own personality and the personalities of those that you work with and care for. In yet another amazing book, *The Four Tendencies: The Indispensable Personality Profiles That Reveal How to Make Your Life Better*, Rubin gives you a great, quick read and an even quicker quiz that lets you know your personality tendency. You can even take the quiz by heading to her website.[7] Here is my version of the four personality types based on Gretchen's helpful breakdown.

The Four Personality Types

I'LL DO IT MYSELF

This person wants to complete all inside and outside tasks drawing motivation from within, often without help from others.

WHY SHOULD I DO IT?

This person will do what they think is a good idea, but for all actions suggested by others, they want to be able to answer "Why?"

BECAUSE YOU SAID

This person is motivated to do whatever people want them to in order to keep things smooth and peaceful.

I WON'T DO IT

This person isn't looking to do anything they don't want to do and will go out of their way to resist things they want if they think someone else wants them to complete those tasks.

I found this so useful for myself. My personality type is "Because You Said" combined with "I Won't Do It." The former means I am driven by outward expectations. So, if I promise someone I'm going to do something, I am more likely to do it than if I only promise it to myself. That's a pretty interesting discovery for someone who owns her own business to make.

Knowing my tendencies has allowed me to put strategies in place that support me. Namely, inviting accountability partners into my life, hiring a business coach, joining WeWork to get this book written, and creating structure to ensure success. I bet by now you're wondering about the "I Won't Do It" side of my personality. So, let's look at that.

I'm also part "I Won't Do It," because I just don't want to do some things. This only applies to areas of my life that don't directly impact other people: so, my health, how organized my garage is, etc. Once I understood what Rubin teaches in *The Four Tendencies*, it was easy to see that each of the kids I work with has their own tendencies as well.

Knowing that a child was a "Why Should I Do It?" personality type, I also knew that I had to give them a reason why we were doing something to help them get on board. (And yes, this does help adults who have this personality type as well, thanks Gretchen!) The "I Won't Do It" camp needs to think they came up with the idea themselves, so sometimes giving them a few choices works best. "I'll Do It Myself" and "Because You Said" personality types are generally the easy kids, but it's good to know who they are—that way you can always check in with them and even acknowledge the great behavior they always put forth.

We "Because You Said" individuals were the kids that always sat down the first time we were asked to and then had to wait while the "I Won't Do It" and "Why Should I?" friends were still playing. A lot of times, that seemed more like a punishment than an achievement. With that said, make a point to check in on the quiet kids, they may be screaming inside for your love and attention.

What About Love

By now everyone has heard of his book, *The Five Love Languages: The Secret to Love That Lasts*, by Gary Chapman. It's also a quick quiz. Basically, you use it to sort out what your true expression of love is. The number one reason to do this is to understand that your expression may not be the same as someone else's expression! When you don't approach each person with their individual expression, it's as if you are speaking Greek while they're speaking French, and neither of you understands a word even though you are both saying all the right things.

This book is so helpful, *The Five Love Languages* has now been adapted to help parents and children too. I mean, even outside of romance, we love, right? Your love language is how you want to receive love. It's what resonates with you.

Five Practical Ways to Display Love

HEARING POSITIVE ACCOLADES—you feel loved when you are acknowledged through verbal statements. "Thanks for planning a trip," or "Thank you for picking up the groceries," are the beeline to your heart.

ACTUAL HUMAN CONTACT—you feel loved when people touch you. Hugs, playing with your hair, snuggling while watching a movie are all things that feed your soul.

SPENDING MEANINGFUL TIME TOGETHER—you feel loved when people choose to be intentional about the time they spend with you. A coffee date with a friend where your phones are on silent or a night at home talking over a great meal with your partner fills you with warm fuzzies.

DEEDS DONE FOR YOU—you feel loved when people do nice or necessary things for you. Your Dad filling up your car with gas or your girlfriend baking you cookies makes you swoon.

TANGIBLE OFFERINGS—you feel love when people give you presents. A diamond for a birthday, flowers for no occasion, or even a coffee to start the morning off in the office will send your heart a flutter.

In my own words the five love languages are

Hearing Positive Accolades—you feel loved when you are acknowledged through verbal statements. "Thanks for planning a trip," or "Thank you for picking up the groceries," are the beeline to your heart.

Spending Meaningful Time Together—you feel loved when people choose to be intentional about the time they spend with you. A coffee date with a friend where your phones are on silent or a night at home talking over a great meal with your partner fills you with warm fuzzies

Actual Human Contact—you feel loved when people touch you. Hugs, playing with your hair, snuggling while watching a movie are all things that feed your soul.

Deeds Done for You—you feel loved when people do nice or necessary things for you. Your Dad lling up your car with gas or your girlfriend baking you cookies makes you swoon.

Tangible Offerings—you feel love when people give you presents. A diamond for a birthday, flowers for no occasion, or even a coffee to start the morning off in the offic will send your heart a flutter

At the gym, our coaches do take the love language quiz so we know how to better communicate our thanks and appreciation to them. We also discuss the kids and what theirs might be so we can better get across to them. It's a great tool when communicating with children. Sometimes, words don't make a differ nce for people, but a hug or action makes a world of difference. Please note: I almost didn't include this section because of the human contact expression. To be clear, you still need consent before speaking this love language. Never put your hands on anyone without their approval.

In The Arena

I hope this chapter was helpful in understanding the different stages of development and how we need to guide children to success. It is so important that they reach each stage and level through their own practice. It's also imperative that we provide opportunities for the kids in our lives. On the other side of things, we also need to avoid overwhelming them with opportunities.

And finally, we definitely don't need to take those opportunities ourselves on behalf of the child so we can feel like they're progressing. We all learn through conflict and being uncomfortable. Sometimes it's hard as parents to sit outside the arena, but still, let your kids take the stage and figure it out.

Once again, this quote sums up our hopes for the children in our lives better than I could (on my own).

> "The credit belongs to the child who is actually in the arena, whose face is marred by dust and sweat and blood; who strives valiantly; who errs, who comes short again and again, because there is no effort without

error and shortcoming; but who does actually strive to do the deeds; who knows great enthusiasms, the great devotions; who spends themselves in a worthy cause; who at the best knows in the end the triumph of high achievement, and who at the worst, if they fail, at least fails while daring greatly, so that their place shall never be with those cold and timid souls who neither know victory nor defeat."

–Teddy Roosevelt

Poetic license mine.

If you can't already tell, this quote means a lot to me. If you want a print out for yourself (because you like it as much as I do), a PDF is included in the reader resources.

Reader Resources

CHAPTER 4

Where We Are as a Society

While the first two chapters told you a bit about where I'm from, who I am and, in turn, what the gym's mission and purpose are, in this chapter, I want us to talk about where the world is today. Yes, even though I know it's tough. I also know that for a lot of us, it doesn't feel like the good old days exist in our modern lifetimes. We value profit over people, and everyone is being asked to do more than they are capable of whether at home or in their jobs. But at our core as human beings, we crave connection, love, laughter, and, in some ways, a simpler life. Collectively, simpler times may seem to be behind us all, but the pure joys of childhood and seeing things for the first time still exist—*if* we let them.

This book is a call to action to create better lives for our children, drawing from my own observations working with kids over the last 10+ years. It's influenced by different schools of thought, organizations and people I find insightful, not to mention countless books, podcasts, social media outlets, how I was parented as a child, and even how I auntie. And I auntie hard!

Although it's not possible to do a deep dive into every potential scenario that exists as a guardian or caregiver to kids, I will do my best to provide a road map for parents and caretakers to enable children to develop necessary skills and grow to be leaders!

The first step is taking a look at where we are as a world. Just like knowing how a child grows and develops is essential in having the necessary tools to further that growth, it's essential to know what's going on in the world so we can navigate it accordingly. So, where is society as a whole? Not in Kansas anymore, I'll tell you that.

The way I see it, there are four major influences that impact our children and our parenting:

- ☒ Fear
- ☒ Overparenting / Under Disciplining
- ☒ Technology
- ☒ Avoiding Both Conflict & Risk

This is not an exhaustive list. There are a ton of other factors, especially related to each individual's circumstances. However, this list is based on my observations and the topics du jour that people are currently choosing to bring to light. Let's dive in to each one of these influences, shall we?

Fear

Yes, fear. How many of us won't let our children run to the store by themselves or ride bikes with a group of friends to the park because we are afraid of what might happen? Most. Many times, our fears are over the top—having been pulled straight from our favorite crime show. In her book, *How to Raise an Adult: Break Free of the Overparenting Trap and Prepare Your Kids for Success*—which happens to be one of my favorites— Julie Lythcott-Haims talks about the '70s and '80s as being the "stranger danger" decades, where kidnappings seemed rampant and you could be snatched o the street just walking to school.

I clearly remember how we were warned not to put our names on T-shirts or backpacks. Doing so would give power to a stranger that allowed them to pretend to be a friend of the family—and this meant they could kidnap us! My parents gave exactly zero shits about this. I had a custom sweatshirt because it wasn't common to spell Michele with only one 'l.' I remember being with my family in Macy's in New York, headed to see Santa. I had my favorite yellow sweatshirt on, the one I got at the T-shirt Emporium in Westfield, New Jersey. I can still smell the creativity—or was it the hot plastic letters under the press? Regardless, that place was amazing.

Inside of this magical shop, you could get custom shirts made in minutes. I chose the oval iron-on motif with a unicorn, rainbow, and babbling brook. The unicorn's front hooves were outside the frame as if it was running toward you. On the back, my name was emblazoned across my shoulders in fuzzy letters. This was a huge epically big deal to me, as my name—like I said—is spelled uniquely. Now, back to Macy's.

As we walked through the store, someone yelled my name. Walking a little ahead of my parents, I turned to look and realized it wasn't anyone I knew. It was a really tall teenager or grown-man type—at least to my 8-year-old self. He joked and teased, but it stopped me in my tracks because I didn't realize how he knew my name.

Then I remembered.

Insert a light bulb over my childhood head. I don't think my parents were phased in the least bit because frankly, they were sane human beings. I was a little put-off, but what that experience taught me, along with a short discussion with my parents, was to identify strange behavior. Instead of being alarmed by strangers in general, I was able to look at each individual behavior to determine whether it was strange. This meant I wasn't in constant "stranger danger."

But because this is such a huge deal, and fear is such a strong motivator, we need to get more serious. Let's have an honest conversation about statistics and the impact they have on our viewpoints. After that, I want to go one step further to shed light on the interpretation of statistics and the impact they have on our thought process when raising children.

In a report called "National Incidence Studies of Missing, Abducted, Runaway, and Thrownaway Children," also known as the NISMART. There are currently three versions of this report, and in the second one, NISMART-2, which was compiled in 1999, around 797,500 children were reported missing, with 115 of them being victims of long-term abductions that were committed by people outside of their families. It is unfortunate that 40% of the 115 in that group were killed. We also know that according to NISMART-3, which was compiled in 2013, the number of missing persons overall decreased by 31%.[8]

Let's put this data into context. In 1999, the US population was approximately 279 million—71 million of those were children. If 115 of those were victims of stereotypical kidnappings, and 40% of those kidnapping victims were killed, that is an infinitesimal number. Children abducted by strangers represent .01% of all missing children. The other 99.99% of children reported missing have been erroneously thought by caregivers to be missing and were generally taken by family members, ran away, or were thrown away (meaning their families did not want them to return). It is a cruel myth that more and more children are going missing and that most missing children have been abducted by strangers.

Updated reports that came out for 2023 show that while there has been an extremely small uptick in children found in human trafficki   situations[9], according to the population

---

8   U.S. Department of Justice, "National Estimates of Missing Children: Updated Findings from a Survey ...," National Estimates of Missing Children: Updated Findings From a Survey of Parents and Other Primary Caretakers, 2013, https://ojjdp.ojp.gov/sites/g/files/xyckuh176/files/pubs/250089.pdf.

9   United States Census Bureau, "Quick Facts United States Population Percentages 2022," Quick Facts United States Census Bureau, accessed September 9, 2023, https://www.census.gov/quickfacts/fact/table/US/PST045222.

estimates for 2022[10], they still fall below 0.00000017% of the population of children.

Of course, serious harm coming to any child is an unspeakable tragedy, and real child predators are out there, even though very few commit stranger-to-stranger crimes. With all that in mind, we must ask "Why do we base our daily decisions about our children's comings and goings on a one-in-a-million chance that our kid could be killed by a stranger?"

As the Palm Beach Post reported in a 2006 article titled "How Dangerous Is Childhood?" that in any given year, a child is more likely to be killed in an equestrian accident (1 in 297,000), as a result of youth football (1 in 78,260), or as a passenger in a car (1 in 17,625).[11] Yet, these statistics, although they may live in the back of our minds, do not prevent us from encouraging our kids to play sports, nor do we banish the use of cars.

Taking the long view, we need to teach our kids street smarts, like the importance of walking with a friend instead of alone, and how to discern bad strangers from the overwhelming majority of good ones. If we prevent our children from learning how to navigate the world beyond our front yards, it will only come back to haunt them later on when they will feel frightened, bewildered, lost, or confused out on the street.

---

10   The Annie E. Casey Foundation, "Total Population by Child and Adult Populations: Kids Count Data Center," Total population by child and adult populations | KIDS COUNT Data Center, accessed September 23, 2023, https://datacenter.aecf.org/data/tables/99-to-tal-population-by-child-and-adult-populations#detailed/1/any/false/1095,2048,574,1729,37,871,870,573,869,36/39,40,41/416,417.

11   Nicole Neal, "How Dangerous Is Childhood?," Palm Beach Post, August 13, 2006, https://www.gainesville.com/story/news/2006/08/13/how-dangerous-is-childhood/31492915007.

According to the Office o Juvenal Justice and Delinquency Prevention, a division of the Department of Justice, the overall rates of missing children actually decreased signific ntly in 2013 when compared to 1999.[12]

In January of 2021, Reuters published the article, "Kidnapped children make headlines, but abduction is rare in U.S." which states that fewer than 350 people under the age of 21 have actually been abducted by strangers in the United States per each 12-month period since 2010—and that's according to the FBI. Furthermore, from 2010 through 2017, which is the most recent data available, the number has ranged from a low of 303 in 2016 to a high of 384 in 2011. This means there was no clear directional trend.[13]

Hundreds of thousands of juveniles are reported missing to the FBI each year. The circumstance of each disappearance is only recorded about half the time. But in cases where they are, only 0.1% are reported as a child having been abducted by a stranger. The vast majority of missing juveniles, typically more than 95%, ran away from home.

12   Andrea J. Sedlak, David Finkelhor, and J. Michael Brick, "National Estimates of Missing Children: Updated Findings from a Survey of Parents and Other Primary Caretakers," National Estimates of Missing Children: Updated Findings From a Survey of Parents and Other Primary Caretakers, June 17, 2017, https://ojjdp.ojp.gov/library/publications/national-estimates-missing-children-updated-findings-survey-parents-and-other.

13   Reuters Staff, "Kidnapped Children Make Headlines, but Abduction Is Rare in U.S.," Reuters, January 11, 2019, https://www.reuters.com/article/us-wisconsin-missinggirl-data/kidnapped-children-make-headlines-but-abduction-is-rare-in-u-s-idUSKCN1P52BJ.

A US Justice Department study in 2002 reported that 99.8% of children reported missing were found alive.[14]

From a statistics standpoint, kidnapping, a real fear among parents, is less than a nominal threat. Yet, it drives so much decision-making. How do you get past your fears? You face them and you educate yourself and your children to deal with what might come, even if it's statistically impossible. There are so many other fears that drive our decision-making but, in reality, have a low statistical probability of actually happening to your child. Like playing sports or riding in a car.

Consider also what things are worth taking a risk for. Kids fall, they get cut, break bones, and have bloody noses. They will be upset and seemingly regret participating in activities where accidents took place, but that's when you really have to parent. Have conversations about how it's important to always try new things and that even when we fail, it's worth it to try again. As Erikson's stages of development stress, it's in the midst of failure that we're able to learn a better way. Allowing fear to dictate every decision we make creates so much anxiety for us and robs our children of the experiences of being successful in their own rights. Failure allows them to experience conflict and to get to the other side.

Overparenting and Under Disciplining

I know no one wants to admit that they overparent, but most of us do. The days of helicopter parenting are long

---

14   Office of the Inspector General, "The Federal Bureau of Investigation's Efforts to Combat Crimes Against Children," OIG Audit Report 09-08, September 2008, https://oig.justice.gov/reports/FBI/a0908/chapter3.htm.

gone because instead, parents are usually either bulldozing or gentle parenting.

Bulldozer parenting is exactly what it sounds like: Parents plow the path and illuminate all conflicts and obstacles in the way of their child or children. Remember Erikson's Chart? Growth from each stage of development happens inside of conflict. If your child never experiences conflict, how will they solve problems, trust themselves, have any confidence, or be able to do anything without your assistance? You may think you are creating a great life for them, but you are actually dumbing them down to the point that they have no real goals or ambitions. Did you ever notice when you don't have a purpose that you get a little sad and even depressed? Imagine being a kid and not having the opportunity to even explore to see what you like to do and never finding anything on your own? We need to let kids find their own way.

Gentle parenting encompasses four pillars. Empathy, respect, understanding, and boundaries when raising your child. The issue is, most people leave out the last pillar, boundaries, so their version of gentle parenting looks more like tyranny by a toddler and that trend continues throughout the years. Kids need boundaries: They crave them. We'll talk more about boundaries in a minute, but for now, I'd love to tell you a lesson in parenting I experienced firsthand from the wild and wonderful world of animals.

A Lesson From the Animal Kingdom

So, I lived in a great rent stabilized apartment in the Greenpoint neighborhood of Brooklyn, New York for 13 years. By the time you read this book, I will have started Act

3 of my existence, which will be based in Colorado. In the time that I lived in Greenpoint, without fail, every winter, the mice came!

One year, well into spring, I caught one. But, of course, it wasn't just that solo mouse hanging out in my house. They say for every one you see, there are seven lurking around! The next thing you know, I have mice running all over my apartment like they were drunk and had no idea how to act. I even looked on the arm of my couch and a tiny one was staring up at me, as if waiting for me to bring him a tiny chunk of cheese on a mouse-sized plate.

Lucky for me, I had a friend smart and brave enough to come over and wrangle them. While they were doing that, I had to leave the house. I will squish a roach in between my bare fingers without any problem or a second thought. But do not even ask me to dispose of a *dead* mouse in a trap. I'll shiver in disgust just thinking about it.

My friend told me that the mice running all willy-nilly around my apartment were babies and they just didn't know how to be mice at that point. And without a mama, well, they were feral. The one I had caught was the mama mouse—the one responsible for raising and training these little ones. Report me to PETA for killing a mouse if you must, but I stand firm on doing what had to be done to reclaim my home.

Most offspring in the animal kingdom need a mama or dada, or a surrogate parent, to teach them how to be the animal that they are. The elder cultivates their instincts and provides nature's boundaries. Children need the same thing. In fact, like I mentioned in the last section, they crave boundaries.

Kids don't need their parent or guardian to act like a friend. They need someone who is going to provide a safe space, give them clear expectations, and show appropriate love and care. Imagine growing up where there were no boundaries. Your parents let you eat whatever you wanted whenever you wanted, no one ever shared a meal together, and you never had to clean up after yourself. Would you feel safe leading yourself through life as a child of 3, 4, 5 or even 10? Hell no.

Kids are always going to test you. Yes, parenting is challenging. Just like coaching and executing a balance beam routine, you need to be relentless in your teaching both to help your athlete execute a successful event and keep them safe. By that, I mean it is vital to stay the course. Resist giving in to the little things so that you can create necessary boundaries for your child and yourself.

Your child is forever going to push the envelope to assert their independence. There will be moments when you present the option to extend those boundaries as they grow, but giving in to their every desire and whim is only going to create chaos in your life and theirs.

It's a fine balance, but it's a balance you absolutely can find. Throughout the book, you'll see little gems on how to find balance. Every situation is different, so always think of your why. Make sure to listen to your inner compass and look ahead to the end game. Will the choice I'm making today forward the conversation of my child's independence, emotional well-being, and success as a human being? It's okay to fail or give in on occasion: I mean we all need the noise to stop sometimes! Just be sure to get back on track and stay committed to the future.

Technology

The truth is, technology is awesome: It's also a bitch. Life has become so convenient because of advances in technology. Time has been freed up, but are we using those additions of time wisely each day? Even having both a washing machine and a dishwasher saves us countless hours a week. Shows on demand, answers at our fingertips, and being reachable at any time are things that have all combined in ways that have almost eliminated any opportunities for us to learn and retain basic life skills. How? I'm glad to explain. You see, when I was a kid, we made mixtapes.

After School, I'd go to Cathie's house (she's still one of my besties) and we'd put a clean tape in one slot of her tape deck. Then, we would turn on the radio. Cathie had a stereo that looked like separate components, but was actually one piece. It held a dual cassette deck, a radio tuner, and a record player on top.

We would sit in her room all afternoon and tape songs that we liked off the radio. While that happened, we would pray that the DJ would let the whole song play, or at least keep their mouth shut until the actual end of the song. We'd have to listen and wait for the songs that we wanted and hope Cathie's mom didn't come in, wanting to tell us what chores had to be done while we recorded on the tape. The chores soundtrack was not one of the desired songs for any of our mixtape playlists.

Sometimes it would take us days to make a mixtape! DAYS. Now, kids can just create playlists on streaming services—in seconds. Oh, and to find out the name of a song and the performer, we'd have to sit and listen patiently, hoping the DJ was kind enough to tell us (after the song was finished recording, of course)!

Now, SHAZAM (literally and figuratively)—you find out in seconds. Why am I telling you about our music-collecting experience compared to modern-day music listening? Because, while technology is great, we learned valuable lessons in Cathie's room in the house across from Roosevelt Junior High School including patience and planning. We learned how to entertain ourselves in between songs and how to compromise on what songs we even wanted to go onto the tape. We got the opportunity to spend countless hours together chatting and being kids.

There is even a difference between what we had as far as TV and games back then. Shows, movies, and video games were only available at home. On car rides, we played the license plate game and bartered with our parents for kids' music time. And when we got a ride home from school, which was a rare break from walking in gaggles together, our parents would talk to us.

On the nights we got to watch TV, I remember running from the basement rec room to my room on the second floor to change into my pajamas during a commercial, racing to make it back before the show started again. Will any kid know the joy of entering the room at just the right time? It was a test, a game we played, to challenge ourselves. And it was a bartering chip for our parents. "Yeah," they said, "you can watch, but you have to do all this stuff in between the commercials." *Hell yeah*, we thought, because we were up for the challenge.

Plus, we (and that "we" includes our parents) weren't reachable at all hours because smart phones didn't exist. And cell phones looked like bricks and were expensive. We left the house in the summer and had to be home before the street lights went on. Then, after the street lights were on and dinner was eaten, we could go back out. But, we were restricted to ghost in the graveyard and manhunt in the backyards on our side of the block. Plus, yards didn't have fences, at least not ones you couldn't easily scale over in a single leap.

Avoiding Conflict & Giving Into Risk Aversion

Going on ten years now, those in the kid industry have been talking about how parents are more and more risk-averse. Now, it's gotten to the point that the focus behind being risk-averse isn't really about the safety of the child, but rather about avoiding judgment from other parents. Social media has made shaming others an everyday occurrence that laptop warriors take very seriously. Check yourself. If you aren't brave enough to share your concerns with someone in the moment, face to face, then you should just keep on scrolling.

One time, I was visiting an online mommy group where a concerned parent posted a picture of a nanny with her twin charges all asleep in the playroom of a high-rise apartment building. It was really a post to bring awareness to how awful that nanny was—sleeping on the job. Insert eye roll. I kept scrolling, but was so annoyed by the presumptions that "concerned citizens" made about the situation.

Firstly, the children were buckled in their stroller facing the nanny. The nanny was an older woman. The scenarios that went through my head were: maybe that's the agreement the parent has with the caregiver, she can rest when the toddlers are resting; maybe workers were in the apartment and this was the only place the kids could have a nap; or maybe this caregiver was up all night with her own sick child and needed to close her eyes for a moment. Also, maybe it's none of your business. No one was in danger. I wish people would stop taking photos of people and posting about them without any context.

Shame, by the way, is often defined as a distressing feeling that results from having done something wrong or socially unacceptable. Brené Brown, my friend, the shame researcher, defines shame as an emotion related to feeling unworthy of love or connection to people or a community as a human, and is always associated with suffering. Both feeling unworthy of love and feeling a lack of connection to a community involve incredible emotional pain. Shame is where we feel *we are* something rather than we did something.[15]

Now, everyone is using phrases like, "I didn't mean to gift shame you." Meaning that when you share about the gifts you receive on social media (what happened to the handwritten note card? Am I right?), someone who

---

15   Brené Brown, "Shame vs. Guilt," Brené Brown, October 10, 2023, https://brenebrown.com/articles/2013/01/15/shame-v-guilt/.

didn't give a gift might then feel shame. Um, what in the actual *@$%. You determine your shame and guilt. Neither is an emotion that someone can make you feel or adopt.

I was a very emotional child and would cry and cry. I felt things so deeply. My Dad, being the child psychologist he was, would say to me over and over, "Michele, no one can make you feel any particular way. That is your choice." I never really understood what he meant back then because the emotions were so raw and real to me. But, as I got older, I recognized that people and kids can be unkind—assholes if you will—but in the end it is my choice if I'm going to let that define how I see myself. Plus, I get to choose which emotions I feel as a result.

So, stop thinking that someone has the power to shame you. You have the power to tell them to f-off. It is important to address shame with our kids because they will definitely face it. And we have the opportunity to teach them, at a young age, that they can work through those feelings.

And for those of you running around mom-shaming women or anything like that, why in the world would you want someone to feel they are unworthy of love, connection, and belonging? Does that make you feel good about yourself? Knock it off.

Can you sense my frustration? My eyes roll a lot when someone attempts to shame someone else during a conversation. I think that often, it's a misplacement of responsibility. Instead of bearing the burden of shame on yourself or harshly judging others, lead with kindness. Be kind to yourself when you have hiccups and feel glaring eyes on you and be kind toward others when they misstep. Hell, extend a helping hand, we are all in this together.

Come from a place of love, always love. And take a minute to refl ct on how modeling this for your kids will help them learn to stop others from playing the shame-game in their own lives.

CHAPTER 5

The Importance of Play

PLAY—self-guided, no adult, good old fashioned FREE PLAY is what I want to talk about in this chapter! But first we need to talk about what happens before kids are able to actively engage in free play. In 2018, The American Academy of Pediatrics (AAP) published an article entitled: "Simple Prescription: Pediatricians Have Role in Promoting Healthy Development Through Play" that encourages Pediatricians to actually write a prescription to parents during wellness visits continually for up to two years for these parents to play with their children regularly![16]

The AAP recognizes the benefits of play and emphasizes that cognitive learning happens during play. Remember Piaget's chart? They recommend playing with children up

---

16   Alyson Sulaski Wyckoff, ed., "Simple Prescription: Pediatricians Have Role in Promoting Healthy Development through Play," Publications.aap.org, August 20, 2018, https://publications.aap.org/aap-news/news/13532/Simple-prescription-Pediatricians-have-role-in.

to the age of 2 because before that, children don't actually know what activities to do or how to engage with others: They need help. Remember the mice? Playing with them until they are 2 years old gives them that stepping stone they need before they can engage in free play.

After that age, a child knows how to play, to inquire, and to try things out! Now, I'm not saying don't ever play with your child again after age 2, I'm just saying they know how at this point and it's important to give them time for independent play without you.

As children grow, free play and recess both become essential. According to Dr. Michael Yogman, young children learn more important skills through play than they do when compared to other school curriculum, and play is more important when it comes to succeeding later in life. He also found that play builds soft skills, which are vital, including being able to collaborate, solve problems, and think in creative ways.[17]

So, I'm all for universal prekindergarten (pre-K) for 3- and 4-year-old kids. And I also believe that we should provide affordable childcare options to families, but let's be sure that these programs are providing the necessary learning tools for children to actually develop. Pre-K, at its best, needs to be more than just an academic setting with rigid rules, course curriculum, and no play!

Children aren't mandated to go to school in Sweden until they are 6 years old. Why? Well going back to the ancient times of Plato, letting kids get their wiggles out

---

17   Michael Yogman et al., "The Power of Play: A Pediatric Role in En-
hancing Development in Young Children," Publications.aap.org, September 1, 2018, https://publications.aap.org/pediatrics/article/142/3/
e20182058/38649/The-Power-of-Play-A-Pediatric-Role-in-Enhanc-
ing.

while they also learn through play in an organic way during their early years is important. It sets them up for success in the classroom later because this is where they are taught to sit still and concentrate.

Findings show that kids that entered school later catch up within the first two years of formal education but with the added benefit of social-emotional growth, learned self-regulation, cognitive awareness, and language that are amassed during early childhood play. To learn more about this phenomenon, I recommend a fantastic podcast hosted by Dr. Kelly Starrett, DPT, and Juliet Starrett, Esq. called *The Ready State*. They are movement gurus. In episode 5 of season 3, which came out December 7th, 2018 they speak with Gray Cook, the founder of Functional Movement Systems. The episode discusses the state of children's health and the aspects that are absent from the global community's agreement about the movements of children after they grow past the age of 21 months. It's a great listen so have at it.

As you can see, this chatter started in 2018, well before schools went remote and children were isolated from their peers for a period of time due to COVID 19. If play being absent was already an issue then, what condition are we in now? Just something to think about. The LEGO® Foundation, in partnership with the Weitzman Institute, rebooted its "Prescription for Play" initiative in 2022 as a result of the impact of the pandemic. The program encourages learning through play by supplying free DUPLO® brick kits and educational materials to different pediatric health care providers. These providers then deliver the materials to patients ranging in age from 18- to 36-months old during routine wellness visits. The LEGO® Foundation is an amazing resource for parents and educators discussing the importance of play, so be sure to take a look at their site for more incredible resources and information.[18]

Outside Play is Also Important

In addition to such initiatives, the focus of play has shifted to include outdoor activities as well. Kids spend hours at school with limited outdoor time and then often go to after-school activities where they are inside for about another three hours. At the gym, we focus on spending as much time outside as possible, including during the winter. One of my favorite sayings is, "There is no bad weather, only bad clothing."

The Scandinavians who said that had it right! It is never a bad day to go outside if you are dressed appropriately. Rain definitely sucks if you have no raincoat and your shoes and socks are wet. I mean most kids don't care, but I do. Those living in NYC have to dress for the weather as they can end up in the elements waiting for public transportation and getting to and from said transportation. And let's face it, NYC is a walking city so everyone in it is always at the mercy of the elements.

Umbrellas are not the most city-friendly accouterment when bustling around, already carrying your bag and whatever else you have with you. When I finally invested in proper rainboots and a hooded slicker my life was instantly transformed! This is why it's important to invest in good outdoor clothing for both you and your kids.

I know, kids grow so fast. It takes money and effort to find the right outdoor gear for a child to only have them

---

18   To visit the The LEGO® Foundation's website, head to https://learningthroughplay.com/about-us/the-lego-foundation

not fit into it the following year. I hear you. My suggestion is to find a kids consignment shop or a thrift store like GoodWill. There is a fantastic shop in my old neighborhood called Parachute Brooklyn. It sells online as well, so Google them and see what you can find. Then, when the item gets outgrown in your house, you can take those clothes in for cash or in-store credit. They aren't the only ones doing such good work.

Check out your community swaps too. A lot of local organizations set up kid and baby clothing swaps and bike swaps! If you can't find one, make your own. Contact your child's school, your community center, or your local municipality to help with the details and space. Another great resource is the Buy Nothing groups on Facebook. Investing time now in researching where to get or trade for clothes can save so much money later.

Even in bad weather, our after school program is outside—at least for the walk to the gym from the school. Daily, we pick kids up from two local schools and walk back to the gym. One school is about half a mile away. A lot of kids actually get bussed to that school from near the gym in the morning. I get it, people work and parents are busy and kids are slow-ass walkers, but it's still important to walk.

When you walk to and from school, not only are you and the kids getting exercise, (each kid should be carrying their own backpack of course), and spending time outside (early morning light helps with sleep and circadian rhythm), but it's an opportunity for you to connect with your child or children. Our coaches learn so much about kids on the walk. They ask questions like "What was the silliest thing that happened at school today?" The walk is also a time when coaches can see if a child is having a hard day or an exceptionally fantastic day. It allows for a deeper connection with a child. And, for you, it can be a source of uninterrupted quality time with your little.

All that being said, here are a few words of advice: Give yourself enough time to walk so you aren't rushing. Generally, whatever amount of time Google Maps tell me it will take to get somewhere, I take and add 50% more time when traveling with children. After all, if you aren't early, you are late. Removing the potential time crunch makes for a much more enjoyable experience. It's okay to slow your life down to a child's pace.

I have had a parent or two ask if we bus the kids in the winter. Um, do you know how expensive a school bus is? And it's only a half a mile. My response when parents say it's cold in the winter is: "Yes, it is, so your child should be dressed for the weather." Then I go on to point out the benefits of the time outside. The walk to the gym is an opportunity for kids to decompress, creating a natural separation between school and afternoon activities. It's a reboot. And honestly, it's fun! Kids take turns leading the group and enjoy racing to the next corner—all while they chitchat with friends who were not in class with them earlier.

It's also important to note that a lot of urban schools provide bussing a certain distance from the school, but only up to certain grade levels. In New York City (NYC) it's third grade. In this particular situation, my suggestion is not to sign them up for a bus, ever! In Kindergarten through 3rd grade, the kids will be bussed, and then poof, at 4th grade the district thinks they should be strong enough, resilient enough, and tenacious enough to manage the walk. The problem is, they haven't been practicing. And for four years the littles have been conditioned to believe it's too hard, too far, and generally undoable.

This line of thinking is consistent with many aspects of child-rearing. Avoiding hard, inconvenient things doesn't prepare kids for anything. It actually makes it more difficul for parents and caretakers to switch the script later. Conflict avoidance serves no one. Ahem, which we can see on Erikson's chart.

Free Play for the Win

Every day in our program, we prioritize free play. Now, we are a gym, and we rent from CrossFit Gantry (thanks Jay and Christina for all your support over the years). It's like a giant jungle gym for adults! Imagine the amazement for kids!

This is the stage area, where the kids eat their snacks, do homework if they like, color, create art and hang out.

We have a huge garage door that is open unless it is below 40 degrees outside.

The rig is a giant jungle gym with rings to swing on.

We also have fort builders, rope swingers, and so much other creative play. None of what the kids are using is actually kids' play stuff. It's just stuff they find purpose with during their play. Read that again.

Free play is just that: It is time for kids to play whatever they want, either with their peers or alone—and with no adult leadership. Do issues arise? Of course, but remember that free play allows for organic development of self-esteem, self-confidence, relationships, leadership, and conflict resolution

Now, do we get involved if they can't sort out a problem? Sure, after they give it three quality tries on their own first. Do we have to teach them how to communicate sometimes and stick up for themselves? Of course. Remember that kids are sponges and sometimes need concepts or ideas to soak up. In going through this process, is there value for the kids? Yes, 1,000 percent. When working through these processes, the confidence the child develops will carry over into everything they do.

Unlike adults, kids don't compartmentalize their success, they are *awesome* in all circumstances, not just inside the gym.

Creating Opportunities for Free Play Outside the Gym

So, you don't have a gym at home. Yeah, I get it. However, you still have options. Look in your community for purposeful free play opportunities. In NYC, since 2016, there has been an amazing organization called play:groundNYC.[19] They are

19   To find out more about play:groundNYC, visit their website at https://www.play-ground.nyc/our-history

a not-for-profit that offers camps and other initiatives in NYC that provides adventure playgrounds for kids.

The Yard, play:groundNYC's home base, is located on Governors Island, a quick ferry ride from the boroughs. This island has no cars and is a biking paradise! The Yard itself pretty much looks like a junkyard or construction site. There are tons of cardboard, wood, and found objects. There is also a tree house, a tire swing, a station with paint, and area with chalk—you name it. The purpose is to let kids play!

The area is for 6- to 19-year-olds and does not allow adults!!! That's right, you have to drop off your kid and go. You can watch, but it's better if you just leave. This is an example of risky play at its finest! Yes, the area is staffed with trained professionals, but this is a wild adventure playground—and it's free.

Adventure playgrounds have been around since the '30s, with many in NYC being built in the '70s—and then shit got weird, or we did. Everyone got scared, and opportunities for kids to play freely evaporated. See the previous section on fear-based decision-making and "stranger danger". But anyway, do some research to see if your community has an adventure playground. If not, you can simulate the same thing in your own backyard. Find your people and invite their kids to come over to play with your offspring.

Infinite Play

Our gym, The Yard, and other programs promote infinite play. Infinite play, like infinite thinking, sees endless possibilities. Finite play, like finite thinking, only has a few possibilities until completion. It always has an end. Even a second start from the beginning leads down the same path. So, what does infinite play look like in practice

LEGO®, especially in its early years, promoted infinite play. Those little bricks provided hours of creative opportunities and challenges to build the tallest tower, the fastest car, or whatever one's heart desired. LEGO® now sells sets. I mean they are amazing, but they are finite. I was fooled by my friend's kids into being excited about Legos, something that brought so much joy to me as a child, only to find out they like building the sets

This experience was tense and a tad bit frustrating as we tried to match the picture instructions to our build. Then, when it was done, we didn't even play with it! They put it on a shelf next to their 12,000 participation trophies. What in the actual *&#%?

They never take them apart and never play with them again. Yes, there is value in following directions and putting things together, but that's not the only way to learn or play. I know so many people that are model builders, but meh, one and done is not worth my money and it stifl s a child's learning, critical thinking, and thirst for knowledge. I'm not saying to outlaw sets and models, I'm just saying to diversify!

Think about what made you happy as a kid, or what made your parents happy when they were kids—or even your grandparents (as I seem to be getting older and older). Think about your young children before they were swayed by marketing masters and school chums with the latest fads. Your baby loved whacking a wooden spoon on the pot. Your mom and dad had jacks and marbles, chalk to draw a hopscotch board, and rocks. Yes rocks! One of the favorite family stories is that my Dad put on a cape when he was probably around 8 years old and jumped off the porch of his childhood home because he thought he could fly like Superman! Little did he know, the towel or bedding he used didn't give him superpowers. If you know my Dad though, you'd agree he is in fact the Man of Steel. Love you, Dad.

Me? I had Lincoln Logs, Legos, dolls, and action figures. (I wasn't allowed to have Barbies, but I did have a Marie Osmond doll, her being a career gal and all. As an aside, I think my progressive parents would approve of the newest Barbie movie, as it makes gentle waves in the world. I also had my bike, balls, hula hoops, a baseball glove, a school playground, a new set of 64 Crayola Crayons (with the sharpener of course), blank paper, markers, and other kids for outdoor games like freeze tag, manhunt, baseball—you get the picture! We also loved finding shit in the garage

I was an outside kid for the most part and the day our family or a neighbor got a new appliance was *amazing*! The commodity that is a giant cardboard box attracted kids from a five-block radius! Big boxes mean it was time to build a time machine or even better a *rocket ship* —outside, on someone's lawn, of course.

Free Play Promotes Better Decision-Making

Stop asking your kids what they want to do. I'm not saying you should tell them what it is they want, but limit your influence to curating their choices. Younger children may even need help setting up certain activities. Plan to provide suitable options for them to choose from and they will find something. An iPad or TV are not suitable choices for free play. Too much screen time in general can be a roadblock to prioritizing play as per the 2018 initiative toward prescriptive play.[20]

And if your child says those cursed words, "I'm bored!" do like I do and waive your arm like you're presenting the showcase on the *Price is Right* and say, "Sounds like an

---

20   Alyson Sulaski Wyckoff, ed., "Simple Prescription: Pediatricians Have Role in Promoting Healthy Development through Play," Publications.aap.org, August 20, 2018, https://publications.aap.org/aap-news/news/13532/Simple-prescription-Pediatricians-have-role-in.

opportunity for fun!" Parenting hack: Hold onto those old boxes. I have a friend whose daughter made a "food truck" out of a large box and played with it every day for over a week. It cost them *nothing*, and occupied her daily for a long time!

But what about play during the school day? Keep in mind that physical education (PE) class, or gym, as we like to call it, and recess are not the same. I'll say it again for the people in the back: PE Class and Recess are NOT the same! And for that matter, neither are organized sports like being on a soccer or basketball team.

PE Class is an academic subject. Yes, you read that right, *academic*. How? Because PE is a class being taught by an adult with the intention of translating skills and facilitating sports and games in a structured setting. Academic by definition is "pertaining to education and study.

Team sports are also structured play. The benefits are outstanding, but are also notably different from those gained by free play. Now, what about recess is "pertaining to education and study"? Not a whole lot. Recess is a break from normal duties. A ten-minute recess will happen in court, and a 30-minute recess might happen during school.

This means that no teaching or adult leadership should occur during recess! Although recess and PE may seem interchangeable, their functions and motivations are totally different. Eliminating one of them for the other can have lasting effects.

Recess gives kids an opportunity to decompress, leave the watchful eye of an adult, and use their pure imaginations. Recess, when conducted properly, is free play—and free play is gold! This is where kids can be kids unobstructed by adult influences. It's where they learn to negotiate, become leaders, use their imaginations, run wild, resolve conflicts, and organically develop other important life skills. It's the continuation of early childhood learning.

Yes, recess, PE, and organized team sports are cut from the same cloth in the sense that they all focus on movement and physicality for kids. However, their purposes and intents are drastically different. Again, PE is structured, adult-led, movement- and skill-oriented, and rules-driven. Recess is relaxation, unstructured, autonomous, child-led, and a break from school. They all have their place.

Too many schools do not have enough recess for children. The younger the child, the more brain breaks they need. Of the schools that still have recess, too many have decreased the amount of recess time, compressed it with lunch hours, or hired companies to facilitate and manage it. Some even use recess as a disciplinary tool. Stop taking recess away to manage behavior issues in the classroom! This all defeats the purpose and makes recess a chore or something you have to earn rather than the reset it is intended to be.

And before you go there, yes, unstructured play and child-led play can also bring up problems. Name-calling, injuries, arguments, and the like can ensue, but that is life. Oh, close your mouth, I don't mean that is life and those are the breaks kids, I mean that is life—where there are trials and tribulations and conflict. It's in those moments that we as adults intervene to teach and guide children to deal with things. But be wary when you are fixing situations and the kids aren't involved in the process.

Conflict, as you recall from Erikson's psychosocial development stages, is also an opportunity to help children develop coping skills and mechanisms to get through these stages. Let them manage it.

If you are asking, "How will I know when to get involved?" Oh, you'll know. We have created a culture of children that run to adults to manage their problems. (I know some adults like that too, but I digress.) Kids will most definitely tell you when there is an issue. It's your job as an adult to teach them the skills to handle it themselves. Our inherent reaction is to protect children, but when they don't have opportunities to learn how to handle difficul situations, we are technically protecting them from learning to manage unjust situations, including their own feelings and emotions. So, next time something happens—because again, it's life and something *will* happen—we want them to be able to deal with it themselves.

Planning Ahead & Thinking Through Responses

Yes, we're advocating for children to learn how to handle situations in safe spaces, but adults still have work to do, too. Adults should have a plan of how they are going to deal with arising issues.

During our free play (or recess) period at our after-school program, when a child comes to me with a complaint, I firs acknowledge their feelings. For example, I might say, "Wow you are really upset/mad/annoyed by that, aren't you?" Then I ask what they said to the person after the egregious action occurred. At the beginning of the year, 90% of them say, "I didn't say/do anything." My response is, "Well if someone said/did X, Y , Z to me, I would tell them what they did wasn't very nice, I didn't like it, and not to do it again." I would then send them on their way to set their own boundaries about how they would like to be treated.

Most of the time, this solves the problem for the afflicte party. It's not so much the doing that bothered them, but how it made them feel. When they then articulate that upset emotion to their peer and advocate for themselves, they get their power back. It's amazing to watch, and that one action may potentially put the aggressor in his or her place!

Now, there are kids with consistent behavior problems. I'm not talking about Individualized Education Plan or Programming (IEP) or diagnosed challenges; I'm talking about kids that can just be jerks at times. They seem to be the ones whose behavior challenges everyone, including me. Sometimes conversations work and sometimes actions work. Most young kids have a disconnect between what they do and what gets done to them—and you need to draw the dotted line for them.

Piaget's cognitive stages lay this out for us. For instance, one child I know enjoys knocking forts down. One day, he ran up to me to tell me someone knocked his fort down. I let him go on and explain everything to me. I said, "Wow that must feel pretty bad since you worked so hard on it." I too went on and on about his feelings, validating them in the moment.

Once he was a little calmer and more receptive, I said, "I wonder if that's how the other kids feel when you knock down their forts?" Deadpan, the 8-year-old looks at me and goes, "Oh." It was like a light bulb went on in that very moment.

Did it change his behavior all the time? No. Did it improve his behavior overall? Yes. Is destructive play a form of play that can happen without the malicious intent of being an asshole to others? Yes. Is there a way to manage that malicious intent when it pops up? Yes. Do we, as adults, have to intervene and assist in those instances? The answer is also yes.

What About the Importance of Play in Team Sports?

That's a great question. I was a soccer player growing up. I also played softball. And during summer break, I didn't play any sports. Soccer was not year-round. The intensity of team sports these days is doing more harm than good in a lot of instances. Kids are overworked mentally and physically and, in the end, they quit. If you watch the documentary *In Search of Greatness*, you'll see that Gretzky, Rice, and Pelé all became leaders in their sports because of their love for those sports. No one forced them to play.

Gretzky said that when hockey season was over, he threw down his stick and picked up his baseball glove. He also added that one time the parent of a young athlete asked how many hours of practice it would take for their child to become him? He said he didn't know. He lived and breathed hockey because he loved it, not because there was a formula to make him the best.

As a parent, support your child: Don't push them to be something *you* weren't. Also, respect the game, their coaches, the referees, and the rules. I went to see my friend's 8-year-old kid play soccer under the lights at the park one night. A goal was clearly scored when the other team was off sides. Amidst the sighs of injustice from our fans, I said to my friend, "Wait for the ref, he'll call it." Sure enough, the goal was retracted. My friend stared at me in awe and asked how I knew that. I said, "I played soccer."

It occurred to me that half of the parents screaming and yelling on sidelines across the country don't even know how specific sports are played. And, on top of that, a lot of them have been drinking. Listen, I'm all for outdoor adult beverages, but remember where you are and show some restraint. Be an example to your child and encourage them—but, for the love of all that is human—stay in your lane. When parents want to watch classes at the gym we say sure, and let them know that they can be a cheerleader, not a coach. Leave that to the experts. Respect the official and be an example to your child.

Team sports still serve the purposes of teaching kids to initiate teamwork, develop communication skills, use critical thinking, exercise, engage with their community, practice discipline, and build confid nce to name a few. Not to mention create a great work ethic. Keep these in mind and if your child isn't getting the bene ts, it's time to supplement team sports with down time for regular free play.

A Place for Play

Now that you know about the different types of play, when and where they happen, and how often you should prioritize each, there is also a time and place for responsibility. This too, coupled with play, will help your kids become well-functioning members of your family and society at large. The perk? Your child's increasing independence gives the gift of time to you! Yes, you will have a moment to yourself. So, read on, friend, read on.

CHAPTER 6

Responsibility

We've talked about play: Now let's talk about work. Have you ever asked a child what their job is? I have. My nephew, in his infinite wisdom as a 3-year-old, said to me, "Shelly, my job is to play!" And it's true, each kid's job is to play because, as we discussed, free play is where all the magic happens!

During free play, children learn how to lead, negotiate, compromise, problem solve, share, take risks, resolve conflict, and all the other good stuff. And where there is play, there is work. In my humble opinion, what seems like work to us, to kids is really just structured play (and this includes chores). After all, play is learning. Task-oriented actions provide their own benefits, like learning necessary skills, but they also help the child understand that they are an integral part of a family and they too can contribute regardless of their size and age.

A major principle in the Montessori method is incorporating chores. The belief is that when children complete daily or weekly tasks inside the home, they will gain a feeling of self-directed purpose. This creates a growing sense in them that they are contributing to the family, which can bring forth the desire to do things that benefit others. This is something they can take with them on their journeys through the rest of life.[21]

Start 'em young, they say. I happen to agree because it's easier to create habits and introduce necessary skills into a young life than to try to make them do things they may not like or see value in later—you know, when they could be doing fun stuff. For example, every Saturday morning, my brother and I would rise with the sun, make cereal, and watch Saturday morning cartoons. When I got older, I spent my Saturday mornings in my warm bed, sleeping, which replaced the sacred morning hours of *The Smurfs* and *Laugh Olympics*. If you know, you know. When we no longer got up so early, we would still be expected to get our weekly chores done before noon. There was no more time for lounging.

There was some resentment in "having" to do chores, rather than them just being a part of what we did to contribute to the family. The same is true about exercise. I'm in the gym business, and our goal is to have movement be second nature to kids: not something that is later prescribed by a doctor to manage disease. How hard is it to start a workout program after years of neglecting your body and adopting a sedentary lifestyle? Incredibly hard. Building a great foundation that includes the "love-to-dos" and the "necessities" is essential. Chores provide the basis for developing a great work ethic, helping kids

---

21   Linda Mora, "How Household Chores Can Solidify Your Child's Montessori Education," Montessori Plainfield | Montessori Frankfort, October 12, 2017, https://montessoriofplainfield.net/blog/how-household-chores-can-solidify-your-childs-montessori-education#: :text=Accomplishing%20daily%20or%20weekly%20household,the%20rest%20of%20their%20lives.

take pride in their work, building independence, and learning to manage basic life skills.

"So," you might be wondering, "how young can they start and what exactly can my kid do?" There are always age-appropriate chores. You can easily use Google lists. I remember ironing my Dad's hankies and other easy items in elementary school as one of my chores. I get it that I grew up in the stone age and no one irons anymore, but it was a task I actually loved. Oh, what's a hanky? It's a reusable tissue that most often men carry. My Dad still has one to this day with him at the age of 87. True gentlemen that one.

It was serious business, including a hot iron and all, but kids can handle hard things. A good guide organized by age is also available in our reader resources. These are guidelines and chores can be assigned even if not necessary. I doubt my Mom would have ironed pillow cases if she was doing the task. If you already took a peak, yes, ages 2-3 can do chores: setting the table, folding dishtowels, and picking up toys and games are just a few.

Just for reference, this is an iron

Reader Resources

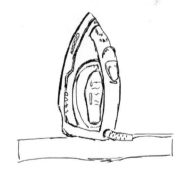

and this is a hanky:

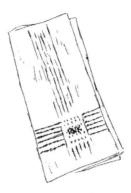

Before we go any further, remember these three things:
1. Have reasonable expectations for what the end results will look like.
2. Make sure related supplies are within reach and properly sized for your little so they have a better chance at being successful at what you ask them to do.
3. Your child is capable of more than you think. Believe in them!

It's true that a child is never going to do a chore as well as you. That doesn't mean they shouldn't do it. Just keep in mind you may have to sweep up again, refold the clothes, or re-rinse the dishes to get all the soap off. When I was probably about 5, my Mom let me wash a few of our favorite character glasses start to finish. While I was doing that, she was making "chocolate shakes" with my brother. They were just made of milk, Hershey's syrup, one banana, and some ice.

Anyway, we used the freshly cleaned glasses to enjoy our treats. We all agreed that the shakes tasted like soap because I had cleaned them so well. I remember we had a good laugh before my Mom rewashed the dishes and we helped her make new chocolate shakes. It's a memory that I look fondly on, so let your kids do the work first. I also always remember folding the towels. It's still way easier folding towels than t-shirts or pants. Adjust the chores to fit your child's age.

Think about these ideas through the lens of this question: Have you ever tried to ride a bike that was too small or too big? You don't get very far on either, right? In fact, it can be near impossible to move on a bike that isn't the right size. The same thing is true when it comes to kids and chores. Asking a 7-year-old child to put the sheets on a king-size bed is a bit daunting. Or, having them put the dishes away when they can't reach the cupboard is going to end in a disaster for everyone, especially the dishes.

First, invest in cleaning tools and supplies for little hands. Next, store items at their height so they are easily accessible and a child can manage things unassisted. This especially includes items that are specific to their lives like water bottles, lunchboxes, storage containers, shoes, socks, hooks for coats, bins for hats and mittens, and the like. The more things are accessible to your child, the more independent they will be in completing a task. This frees up your time too!

Their Contribution to the Family

The purpose of chores is to teach life skills, build confidence and belonging, and inspire independence. When thinking about which chores to give out, you want to create opportunities for kids to succeed. In this case, each accomplishment translates into pride and they radiate. That said, it's okay for a grown-up buddy to help out a bit if a chore is challenging. To this day, my friend will always insist on helping me make my bed, stating, "It's just easier with two people." So very true.

Also keep in mind that your child is more capable than you think. They can sweep, scrub, make beds, put toys away, feed the family pet, rake the lawn, and water plants —just to name a few. Take the time to lay out the parameters and expectations, and teach them how each chore is done. They'll get it and each time they do it after that initial lesson, they will get better. Doing things is the practice that, over time, will create competence and success. If a houseplant is sacrificed in the process, it's okay. The risk is more than worth the reward.

When adding chores to the mix, avoid adding rewards. Helping your family through chores is your child's contribution to the family and to the house. It is unnecessary and even detrimental to pay a child for the work they do that helps the family maintain the house. Paying a child for basic chores is teaching them that they don't have a stake in the game and they should be compensated for what is truly their innate responsibility.

Having them doing unpaid chores is not sending the message that all the work they do should be free, which is what some parents think. Instead, chores without pay sets up the framework that they are already getting something by virtue of being in the family rather than them deserving something for the work they do. As they get older, allowances and conversations about their value in a work environment can be integrated. Don't worry, later on in the book, there is a chapter that includes guidelines for teaching kids fiscal responsibility.

Another great way to instill personal responsibly and pride in your child is to have them take ownership of their personal items and needs. Let them brush their own teeth at a young age. You can always do an extra brush at the end, but give them the chance to put the toothpaste on the brush and get at those chompers. Have them pack their school bag and lay out their own clothes the night before.

Thinking Thoroughly About Food

Packing their school bag and even their lunch has a twofold benefit: They will have a relationship to what's in the bag, where they put things, and what is chosen for lunch. As far as lunch goes, set out parameters like, "You need protein as big as your palm, a complex carb that fits in your cupped hand, fruit or vegetables the size of your fist (that's one serving, they need five for the entire day), and a fat the size of your fingertip." I wouldn't worry too much about the fat since it's already in the foods they eat, but feel free to throw in some avocado for good measure and pure bliss.

What I would prioritize is teaching them to embrace whole foods that come in their own packages and not ultra-processed foods that come in boxes. The latter includes protein bars, "healthy snack" alternatives—or, as I like to call them—candy. Yes, protein bars etc. probably have as much sugar in them as a candy bar does. No sugar-added alternatives just mean that fake sugar is added. Your body can't tell the di erence and will react the same in many instances.

Too many processed foods in children have been shown to throw off their gut biome and impact both their moods and their abilities to sit still or even slow down. It is often said that nutritious food and exercise are the most under-prescribed medications. Start at home and focus on getting proper nutrition for your child.

Now, do I think there is a place for sweet treats and the occasional bag of chips? Sure, but only after you've eaten the good stuff. The nutrition side of parenting is a super hard job. Remember, you do the grocery shopping and you are the adult. Your child is not going to starve if you have a standoff about eating vegetables that ends with you not giving them dessert or them skipping a meal—I promise.

Growing some herbs and even small fruits and vegetables will pique your child's interest in cooking and creating recipes that include the bounty of their hard work. Get creative and stay the course. The best way to have a kid eat properly and get enough exercise is to lead by example. So, take the lead! Model the choices and behaviors you want to instill in your child.

Let Them Do It

Let's go back to the backpack. Having them pack it up is a start. After all, it's your child's property and their responsibility. **Do not carry it for them.** I've witnessed so many parents and caregivers schlepping their kid's belongings to and fro while the child, sometimes bigger than the parent, gleefully walks along carrying nothing. WHYYYY??

Yeah, I get it, I don't want to carry my own shit and I sure as hell don't want to listen to a kid whine about how heavy something is, but every time you act as a Sherpa, you are telling your child that they are the center of the universe and you are simply here to serve them. Thanks to John Sullivan for that gem. John Sullivan is the founder and CEO of Changing the Game Project, a movement to return youth sports to children.[22] Now, an artist is only as good as their tools, so make sure your little has a backpack that fits properly. It's fairly simple: the backpack base should rest at the waist line above the hips. Tighten the straps in the front so the bag doesn't sag or pull on the shoulders.

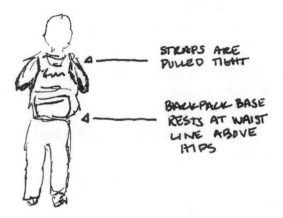

This is so important, and it goes beyond the backpacks too. We literally push and pull our children from place to place as they stay rooted in strollers or on scooters.

The American Academy of Pediatrics says to eliminate strollers by 3 years of age.[23] Most stroller use is about convenience and speed for the rest of us, not the child. Children need to walk and get their footing—literally. So let them. Once they are older, please don't pull or push their scooters. Instead, have them carry their bags and actually use their scooters to propel themselves to get around.

---

22   You can find out more about John and the Changing the Game Project at https://changingthegameproject.com/about/

23   Council on Sports Medicine and Fitness and Council on School Health, "Active Healthy Living: Prevention of Childhood Obesity Through Increased Physical Activity," American Academy of Pediatrics, 2006, https://publications.aap.org/pediatrics/article/117/5/1834/70080/Active-Healthy-Living-Prevention-of-Childhood.

Frankly, I'd skip the scooter and get them on a balance bike first followed by a two-wheeled bike. Children using scooters often favor one side and I'm waiting to hear about the rise in hip issues when these kids all hit their twenties. Or teach them to alternate like my friend who is a Doctor of Physical Therapy (DPT).

While scrolling through Instagram, I saw a post by a former team member of my triathlon days, the aforementioned DPT. It was a short video of his young daughter scooting through NYC. I noticed she would alternate her kick leg when traveling along. I sent a message asking if they taught her that or she did it on her own. He told me how they taught her to do so to create equilibrium and balance to her body. And then he posted about that so other parents would understand why she was scootering the way she was.

My concern, and his as a medical professional, is that favoring one side will impact their musculoskeletal system causing acute or long-term injury. I now challenge the kids to switch legs when scooting and find that balance. It's a hard adaptation after years of single leg scooting, so again, consider the best option may be a balance bike, then a two-wheeled bike.

Next time you are headed to the park or are going out, make sure your child is capable of carrying their favorite stuffy, toy, or game. A small backpack on weekends is great. Start small and be consistent.

Obviously, all of these steps in building responsibility take a little extra time and investment, but I promise, the effort will be worth it. Think about some things you do on a daily basis that you have built into habits. Think about how you feel when you don't do them. I personally didn't start making my bed until I was in my mid-forties. Yep, you read that right. Once I started though, I felt a real sense of accomplishment and a little bit of pride that propelled me to the next to-do on my list.

Some winters in NYC, and especially during the pandemic, keeping to my routine was hard, but it had so much value. Some days, making my bed provided the sense of accomplishment I needed to be happy and productive through those cold and isolating weeks, and it just made my space more organized and inviting. Now, back to Gretchen Rubin's book *Outer Order Inner Calm: Declutter & Organize to Make More Room for Happiness.* The gist is that our environment can and will impact our productivity, happiness, focus and more. The best way to get organized is to have less stuff. This way you don't have to have special boxes or baskets for things, and it's easier to manage in your physical space as well as your head. So don't overwhelm your child with toys and stuff either. Rotate toys, have them donate something when they get something new— and a little lesson in charity gets thrown in. Allow them the mental and physical space to be creative and include them in the development of that space. Honestly, the less there is, then the less there is to clean up!

Bringing that order and satisfaction to my life daily provided room for other things to start happening. My business grew, I exercised more regularly, my artistic hobbies bloomed—these changes meant I was generally happier. I'm not saying making my bed did all of that. I *am* saying that completing that one little task changed how I felt about myself: and there was a snowball effect. When chores and household tasks are a purposeful, managed form of self-care, they will create a new level of respect in you for yourself and your home. Why wouldn't you want to teach that to a child?

I know that many of you have a cleaning person that helps with the maintenance of your home. Trust me, outsourcing is amazing and makes us all happier! I'm sure most of you didn't start life with a cleaning person, and if you did, good for you! I'm being serious, not snarky if you were wondering. It's still a great idea to have a child do chores to learn basic housekeeping skills and to feel that sense of accomplishment and pride. Maybe schedule your child's weekly chores halfway between cleanings so your child's contribution can be seen. That way, what they're doing feels like it has a sense of purpose.

Take a minute to figure out what you can do to help your child build purpose, accomplishment, and altruism into their lives. Use a chores chart, aka a habit tracker, not for tallying tangible or monetary rewards, but to create a concrete showing of all the kid's efforts and hard work then share with them the positive impact of their contribution. A child can look to it and feel satisfied and even share their accomplishments with others. This is important because the tasks and cleaning they do won't be visible each day since things will get dirty again, despite our deepest hopes and desires. Also, make sure to use their love language.

Finally, set aside some time to talk to your child, or use their love language, to relay to them about how they are an important part of the family and can contribute in these ways. Remember too, things won't be perfect, but the experience will be practice for more than just the task at hand. Creating self-sufficien kids who all have great work ethic will give them an edge over others these days.

Independence

Chores and personal responsibility will definit ly create independence among our littles, but they also encourage it outside of the home—out in the real world. The reason for the expression "It takes a village," is that it does. These days, it's less likely that families will live in multi-generational homes with grandparents and babies all together. Today, we are all forging our own paths, and some of us are far from where we started. We have to foster independence by creating opportunities for it, especially for young children. So, in the interest of creating independent kids, let's start by creating a community—aka the previously mentioned village!

In a big city or even a new town, building a supportive village can be daunting. The first thing I'd recommend is to get to know your neighbors in whatever type of community you live in. Neighbors include people who live on your block, the purveyor of your local deli, bodega, or corner store, plus maintenance workers in your apartment or school. Then there's the local librarian and even the crossing guard on their post. Anyone that your family comes in contact with, whether it's close up or even from afar, counts.

In Japan, kids as young as four can be seen riding the subway alone! They wear a yellow cap that alerts the community that they may need assistance. Now, I know, this sounds horrifying, but collective community is so deeply rooted in their culture that this practice is safe and e ective.

Maybe we're not ready for yellow caps and solo-subway rides just yet, though. Let's start small. The reason I say to meet your neighbors is so that you and your child have other touchstones in the neighborhood to go to in the event that you need something or someone. It also creates a comfortable environment for your child where they are grounded and know others. That said, it's important to have ground rules.

People can help when needed, but on your terms. Create the boundaries you are okay with regarding how your child interacts with adults and other members of the community. For example, you might tell your children that it's okay for them to talk to strangers, be polite, and make eye contact, but that they aren't to go anywhere with strangers, let a stranger walk them home, or engage or help them outside of a public area.

For instance, it might be okay for a stranger to help the mom trying to get the stroller up the subway steps, but not okay for them to watch the child or help them up their apartment steps.

Thank a kind soul for offering to carry the grocery bag for you, but let them know you have it. If they persist on carrying it to your home, tell them "No, thanks," sternly and politely and wait for them to leave the store first. Pretend like you forgot something if you have to and go back inside.

The "you" in these instances is a child, but these boundary-setting moments can also apply to adults.

The most important thing is to have a plan for your child to react to different situations. Granted, you can't plan for everything, but having a standard response is helpful when they face a situation that just might not feel right. "Thanks, but my mom is picking me up," or "Thanks, but I've got this," will work just fine

I was recently at a food truck outside of a neighborhood brewery in Denver. The girl in front of me was probably 11 or 12 years old. She left and came back to order after conferring with her parents. Having been privy to her dilemma minutes before, when she came back I asked her in the wide open and in front of other people, "Are you going to get it? There is only one left, and I'll get it if you don't." She just stared at me. When I asked again, she turned away from me. Now before you come to her defense and say she may be dealing with X, Y, and Z, I've been around the block and can discern for the most part neurodivergent souls. I don't think this was the case, considering her table inside was right next to mine and things seemed typical. My point is this child thought or was taught that it was better to ignore people than talk to a stranger. I worry that she won't actually be able to detect a dangerous situation and that she will go on walking around in life completely afraid!

Build the Plan, Talk the Plan

We ride the subway, buses, bikes, and scooters for our camps. We have very specific rules about how we travel: parameters for partners, distance apart, entering and exiting from one door, stopping at every corner, etc. We do go over what a child should do in the event that they are separated from the group.

Always have a plan. Ours is: "Stay where you are. We are coming back for you." We do roll call often and are constantly counting heads, so it will take a mere few minutes to figure out that someone got separated. In the decade-plus that I've been doing this, we had one kid get separated from the group—for two minutes, at a park. And he was ten, not five. We found him so quickly because he stayed put. We explain to the kids that if they move from where we know they are, it will be harder to find them. We also explain that if an adult, a mom or police office offers to take them somewhere, they are to say, "We have a plan. My grown up is coming back here. You can wait with me here." Please note that I used the mom example because I've heard from families that they tell their children if lost to look for a mom in the crowd for help. I'm not against this, but I think it has its flaws.

The last few years, for clarity, we also have them put an ID tag on each of their bags that has our contact information on it along with our plan written out. We practice the scenario and ask questions so the kids are communicating back to us, showing that they understand how it works. Try using this method sometime about anything—have them describe what you just said—it lets you know what kids are really grasping and what is going over their heads. Asking them to say it in their own way clarifies whether or not they truly get it.

The more they understand, the easier it is for them to go o script when asked more questions. Having a plan, as well as prepared statements like in the example above, establishes a level of normalcy and gives each child a task during a time when they could panic instead. Being prepared is a great tool to manage anxiety. Big breaths are followed by "What do I do now?" We teach them to wait. Waiting, although passive, is a job and will give the child a focus rather than wondering what else they should do.

My point is that it's okay to talk to your child about "scary stuff"—the scenarios that you don't want happening, but are afraid might take place. We'll get into this deeper in a future chapter. Coupled with broaching the hard stuff, be sure to tell kids to think about how they feel on the inside and if it doesn't feel right, to fight like hell against whatever is happening.

Everyone has an inner compass that will pull them in the direction that is right for them. However, we must make sure this compass has space to work by refusing to bog children down with illogical actions that are based on senseless fears. Their inner compass needs to point to their true north. If there are a million distractions, the compass will just spin and the child won't identify with anything. When this is the case, kids will only be able to heed what is told to them instead of feeling equipped to make their own decision.

The importance of an inner compass is also for each kid and adult to prioritize their personal safety first. Too many kids I've spoken to say they would feel bad hurting someone to get away from them. Mostly girls, but a lot of kids. I was probably one of them. No one should feel bad about defending their own life. The days of having to fight for survival daily, as it was with our cavepeople ancestors, are gone. But, when we sense danger, we still need to fight like hell.

Independence In Practice

We took a side step from independence and a collective community to address certain underlying fears. So, put into place some family rules when increasing your child's independence. Some may include not going into someone else's house unless they clear it with you. This even includes on Halloween. Another could be saying "no" if an adult asks for their help finding someone or something. Teach them to respond with a simple, "I have to go now" and have them be on their way. For kids of a younger age, walking should occur in groups with friends. You see where I'm going here. Think of a few guidelines like this that would work as baselines for your family. Not responding, as in my story earlier, gives o an air of fear and makes your child vulnerable. Teach them to use their voice and own their power.

Now, let's get back to your child's independence in relation to the people who are part of your tribe. You've created a collective community—a village if you will. Talk with your child about how those people are touchstones and can be counted on to help the child out if needed. But also, do me a favor: let those people know you volunteered them for the job.

At the gym, the local businesses knew that I encouraged our kids to reach out to them if needed and what the parameters of help included. Calling us, calling their parents, letting them sit in the store for a few minutes to feel okay or, even in some instances, to cool off from the heat all fall within those parameters. These relationships extended beyond when the kids were with us at the gym to their lives in the community outside of gym hours.

Remember your child's aunts, uncles, and babysitters. It's important for a child to have a trusted adult in their life other than their parents—and not just for emergencies. These are the folks that your child may come to when they are afraid to approach you. Or if they need a little objective guidance, especially as they get older. Young adults can't always take advice from their parents, but often, they can absorb the same words when spoken from someone else.

My life has come full circle as now I am a sounding board and touchstone for the girls of the fab four babysitting squad. They were born when I was about to go to college, so my interactions with them were fewer than with their elder brothers. So much so, that Carrie actually didn't like me. I know, how could that be? Far from the truth now, the love between us runs deep and real.

Over the years I've fi lded calls about medical concerns when they were in college, fall outs with friends as they grew up, nding true love in themselves and a partner, and career challenges and changes. Plus, we've talked about the really big things like one's value in the world. As a woman, I have worked really hard to curate a friendship and sisterly/parental bond with them where they feel safe talking to me and experience being lifted up. There is no subject that is o limits. Both relationships are unique yet cut from the same cloth. Despite not being their mom, I parented them for so many years. Now is the time that we get to experience "the best friends" phase of parenting. It will come for you too, I promise. It is then that you will also get so much more from your child. Thank you Lizzie and Carrie for giving so much to me.

What other things can kids do to gain some independence? Allow your grade-school child to walk to and from school solo. Do you live far? Then walk with them part way and let them navigate the end solo or with a friend. As the school year progresses, add a little more time to their solo trek. Build up their confidence and your confidence in them day by day. Also, chill. Don't track your kid or ask them to text you when they get to school. If you didn't call in an absence, the school is going to call you. Remember what we talked about earlier, fears regarding kidnappings and the like are negligible compared to what we think.

Another way to create independence is to send your kid out to do an errand. Need a cup of milk? Send them to the neighbors to get it. You can even have them make the call beforehand! Stopping by the store on the way home and only need one or two things? Stay in the car and send the kids in. Draw a map if you have to let to them know where the item is. Remind them to be polite to the cashier and to say hello and thank you.

Have kids order their own meals at a restaurant and ice cream at the shop. The more they interact with people who are, by definition, strangers, the more they will be able to tell the differ nce between strangers and strange behavior. If they never speak to anyone other than you, they will never feel comfortable and capable in the world. Constant protection and management from you are disservices to your child and can lead to unnecessary anxiety.

For example, at the gym, for our birthday parties, we always have the guest of honor and their grown up visit the gym to discuss the event, mostly to figure out which games that will be played, with some backups. Plus, we discuss how the afternoon will go and really give the birthday honoree a sneak peak of the gym. It they have never been there before, having a pre-party visit often eases any concerns as well as paints a picture for the child, which gets them excited for the event. They become vested in their own party.

When we have the child at the gym, we sit next to them and converse with them directly about the games they like and everything else. Lately, parents have been showing up without their child or doing things over the phone. We get it, it's a pain in the butt to find 15 minutes to stop by during the week, but this interaction means so much to your child, and helps us pull off a great event. Having direct conversations about an event where the child is the center of attention really elevates that child's feelings of autonomy, control, and independence.

This is why we take an extra step at the end of every summer that is centered around each child: we send a physical postcard to each camp attendee. The front has a group shot of each week of camp and the content speaks to the child's achievements over the summer. We include a reference or two to what made having them at camp so amazing. I have been beckoned from across the street by kids yelling, "I got your message. I got your message!" It took me a minute to realize they meant the postcard we sent in the mail. Who gets personal mail anymore? This is especially true for kids. That personal touch goes a long way! It's just one other step on the road to independence. Listen for the opportunities, seize them, and if they don't seem to exist: create them yourself! Yes, Harry, you have to order your own ice cream and carry your own stuff.

Independence, Peer Play, and Transportation

The playdate—ugh—the play date. We used to just go outside, knock on the door, and say "Hey, can Kevin come out to play?" Or we'd ride our bikes to the elementary school and see who was hanging out at the playground. The purpose of a playdate is for small children to play together. These events are usually set up by parents. The major problem with this is that now parents are involved every second of every minute. They are involved in the scheduling, but also the snacks and the activities. There isn't much free play involved.

I've also heard that the other parent is expected to stay at the host house during the playdate. So now you don't even get an hour to yourself? It's also become quite the competition between adults, constantly worrying about who is hosting the best experience. Oh. Em. Gee. Drop your kid off, let the kids sort it out, and give them a snack if they ask. Why does everything have to be SO much? See chapter 5 about free play and all of the amazing things it does for developing brains, and please—just let them play.

After a certain age, your child can even orchestrate their own meet-ups. Get a landline again or let them use your phone. Better yet, just send them over to their friend's house. If they can't play, your child will come back and have to find some way to entertain themselves at home. Parents are creating more work for themselves and less free creative play for their kids by holding on to the playdate.

If other parents aren't aligned, then make it generally known that your house is open certain afternoons after school, Saturday mornings, or anytime that you are home. Create an adventure playground in your yard—this will get the kids outside and into free thinking and playing. Kind of like the gym, where we have added more and more free play, especially for the younger kids, because they need it. They are so overscheduled. Recently at an after-school open house, two parents asked, "Free play, what do you mean?

We won't even know what our child is doing?" No, you won't, unless you take the time to ask them. We don't send out updates either. Moving along.

For the love of all that is goodness, please teach your child to ride a bike and tie their shoes (without double bunny ears). A lot of city kids don't know how to ride a bike. My Mom was one of them. She never learned as a kid, tried as an adult, got it, but never felt comfortable. She was never able to feel the sheer joy of pedaling on the open road. As she got older, she wanted a tricycle: you know the ones you see at the beach with a back basket? I'm sorry I couldn't make that dream come true for her. RIP Mama.

I couldn't imagine not knowing how to ride a bike. I taught myself in the backyard. I'm sure my parents helped at first, but I was determined. My 4-year-old self rode that purple bike with a banana seat in circles in the yard until I got it. Riding a bike is just balance—once you get it, you don't lose it. Biking was my ticket to freedom! It was a faster way to get places, and, as I got older, I was allowed to go farther than my feet could imagine. Summertime was the greatest: out on bikes at 9 am and home when the street lights came on. Ahh the '80s.

The motivation for city kids and even suburban kids may not be freedom, because let's face it, who lets their kid run wild on the streets of Anytown, USA anymore? It's still so important for them to learn to ride a bike. While I'm not going to go into detail about it here, it's also important for them to learn how to swim, for a lot of the same reasons and for safety. Besides providing independence, learning to ride a bike teaches children patience, problem solving, bravery, resilience, sheer joy, pride, and accomplishment!

Riding a bike is something that will challenge your child and the payoff is amazing!

Once they start riding, they gain both situational awareness and bike handling skills. Situational awareness means they are looking at the whole picture, not just their feet. Cars, pedestrians, road conditions, weather, etc. Being on a bike means they are also not on their phones or playing video games for twelve hours.

Yes, streets are dangerous and bike lanes are often, in urban areas, cluttered with delivery trucks. So, have them ride on the sidewalk. Kids are allowed to ride on sidewalks in NYC if they are under 12 years old and the diameter of their wheel is less than 26 inches. I'm sure it's the same in other communities too. You can even start sending your kid to school on their bike. Have them lock it up in the bike racks and your morning just got a little freer. Better yet, be like PS 110 in Greenpoint Brooklyn and organize bike-to-school days for the whole community!

Now, every time I point out that your life gets easier when your child gains independence, remember, this is your job as a parent. Your goal is to raise a child that can live independently and freely in the world as an adult in the future. It's important that they learn how to do that under your direction and tutelage. I know it's hard to watch babies grow and get older, but it's necessary. And they will love you even more for being committed to a wonderful life for them. Let them fly—and remind them to take their backpacks.

CHAPTER 8

General Life Skills

When raising independent humans, there are general life skills that need to be taught and learned. We covered basic housekeeping skills in chapter 6 when we discussed chores! The other important life skills that probably aren't being taught extensively in schools are:

- ☒ Health & Wellness—Food and Movement
- ☒ Having Good Hygiene
- ☒ Money Management—Fiscal Responsibility
- ☒ Choosing Kindness

There are more, but these are the big ones for me.

Health & Wellness

This includes both food choices and movement practices. Talking about food is always a little meh. I recognize that there is a tremendous amount of food insecurity in the

United States and access to affordable natural foods is a fairy tale for some. Many people are left with few choices and forced to eat what is available. This includes a vast majority of school-age children who get most of their meals from school.

Since this conversation can seem somewhat elitist off the bat, I want to recognize that I am aware. However, it is still crucial to discuss food so that we all understand the importance of getting the proper nutrients. Food education allows all of us to lobby for changes and seek out alternatives, and even look for organizations that are battling against food insecurity.

So, food. We discussed it a little bit when talking about lunches that your kids can pack for themselves. I cannot iterate enough that we need to be more concerned with what our children, and frankly we, are putting into our bodies. Whole natural foods, or foods that come in their own packages, are healthiest.

I prefer organic when possible, as there are findings showing that pesticides are screwing up our hormones. To be clear, I am not saying organic is more nutrient-based than conventional. I am only speaking to pesticides. Unbalanced hormones can lead to fatigue, weight gain, low mood, and even itchy skin—to name a few. Maybe it's not your child's clothes that are causing sensory challenges, but rather their hormones.

Now, I understand that organic food is more expensive and not accessible to everyone. With that being said, buying local is a great alternative if available. Do your best to eat well as often as you can. Every year, lists like the Dirty Dozen and Clean 15 get updated. Use this as a guideline when choosing conventional over organic or vice versa: if it's an option.

Generally, thin skinned berries, tree fruits like apples and pears, and some greens all make the dirty list, so buy organic if you can. Feel free to buy conventional with hard-skinned fruits like watermelon, avocado, and pineapples. Interestingly, asparagus and kiwi are clean too. This full chart is available in our reader resources.

Reader Resources

It's also important to consider your animal protein sources. There is so much verbiage on packaged goods that it's sometimes hard to tell what the healthy stu   is. All meats and chicken are free of antibiotics when they come to market. That means an animal may have been treated with antibiotics to ward o   disease in its lifetime, but by the time of production, the antibiotics are out of the animal and any residuals are not detectable. This includes milk. For example, when looking at chicken, "Raised without antibiotics" means that antibiotics were never used—even at the chicken hatcheries.[24] There are a lot of nuances in labeling, so educate yourself. It is believed that inappropriate antibiotic use in animals creates antibiotic resistance in consumers.

Now, I'm far from telling you to be a vegetarian. I am on Team Meat and believe animal protein is by far the best

---

24   Trisha Calvo, "What 'no Antibiotics' Claims Really Mean," Consumer Reports, September 10, 2020, https://www.consumerreports.org/overuse-of-antibiotics/what-no-antibiotic-claims-really-mean.

source of protein for proper growth. I have friends who were raised vegetarian for religious and cultural reasons. Their lifestyle is very different than some of my friends who went vegetarian later in life.

Again, do your best to stay away from processed foods and fake meats. They are highly processed and don't provide the essential nutrients necessary for proper growth. That is really what this conversation is about, the specific foods children need to grow and develop. (Not that grown-ups couldn't also improve in this area.) Kids should get enough necessary macronutrients, protein, carbohydrates, and fats from reliable, simple whole forms of food to meet their needs to grow, heal, regulate, and generally be happy.

Consumer Reports put out a great article breaking down food labeling and its meaning. You can find out more by visiting their website.[25]

If you have the time, I recommend reading an amazing book all about this topic, *Real Food, Fake Food: Why You Don't Know What You're Eating and What You Can Do About It* by Larry Olmsted. You'll know it when you see it because it has a giant piece of parmesan cheese on the cover.

It's a long read, but it's also fascinating. This book puts into perspective the reality of the healthy food we consume and how the United States Copyright law impacts food labeling. Weird, I know.

When it comes to food, also make sure to listen to the full story. I learned on a tour of an olive mill in Kalamata, Greece that extra virgin olive oil (EVOO) is the first press of the olives. It's olive oil in its purest form. Virgin olive oil is the second press and is made of disregards that are left

---

25   To visit their website, head to https://www.consumerreports.
org/overuse-of-antibiotics/what-no-antibiotic-claims-really-mean

over from the first press. In further discussion, I learned that EVOO does have a high heat capacity, just not for multiple uses. So, if you are frying, only use the oil once, but otherwise, you're good. Put simply, it's an expensive, single-use frying oil.

Our guide's notes about selecting olive oil were to only buy the oil in a glass bottle, or a tinted bottle (since it will break down in sunlight) and apply it amply to all things. After that, you'd want to rub the spills into your skin. This tour was a great experience and I highly recommend it to everyone. The Olive Route in Kalamata. Tell Dimitra I sent you!

As someone who has worked in the health and fitness industry for so many years, I've been asked countless times for advice about how to get kids to eat better. My answer is always to model the behavior you are encouraging and get the kids involved in preparing food. One of our activities during after school, and during our summer camps, is a weekly cooking class. Children (and adults) that engage in the process of preparing meals are more likely to try new things, appreciate better quality foods, and are frankly more invested in what goes in their bodies. Maybe not on a cerebral level, but on a pride level. Remember those herbs I mentioned growing in chapter 6? Start using them.

What I REALLY want to say to people about nutrition is:

- ☒ Who does the grocery shopping, you or your kid?
- ☒ Sugar is in everything, including those "healthy" treats.
- ☒ Don't expect your child to eat healthier than you.
- ☒ Your house isn't a restaurant: If your kid doesn't like what's for dinner, then I guess they aren't eating. Close up your catering business.

Now, I want to acknowledge that talking about food can be tricky. We don't want to create eating disorders or develop a conversation of scarcity around food, especially when a child comes from a home that experiences food insecurity. When I was a kid, it seemed like my Mom was always on a diet. I have spent the better part of my life having unrealistic expectations for my weight and how my body should look. I also felt a lot of embarrassment about my own body and my Mom's.

On some level, I knew she didn't like her body, so why should I like hers or mine? So much time—years, friends, years—and energy was wasted seeing myself as something that I wasn't—fat and unlovable. I use the word fat because when I was a kid, that was the worst thing that someone could call me. Even though I was a healthy, active kid, I wasn't pencil thin so I thought I was fat. For me, that embodies more than just weight, it's a grotesque disdain for myself. Often, when you see yourself a certain way, eventually you bring that to fruition, so I struggled for years with my weight. I was obese at some points.

My focus as I embrace my fifties is to move every day, get enough protein each day, and wear clothes that fit me (not clothes that I want to fit me). It takes work, and there isn't a day that goes by that I don't think about the perils of food and how I could be better at eating. As if that was actually a thing: Better at eating. You know, like better at breathing. Good God. I don't want those same feelings to be experienced by any child. It's important to model the behavior you want them to have.

Modeling is often silent. Just show them what to do based solely on your actions: no talking or qualifying is needed. If asked, choose to say you aren't having dessert because you are full instead of "I need to lose some pounds," or "Chocolate lava cake is bad for you." Instead, share the joy of the whole foods that you enjoy. You can share things like, "This apple is so crisp and sweet, and adding it to this salad is super tasty."

Also watch how you speak to yourself, in private and in front of your kids. While at the beach this past summer, my friend complimented my body. Her teenage daughter was right next to me and I had to literally close my mouth from preventing a negative comment or defl ctive statement from coming out. I paused and simply said "Thank you." It was practice for me and a great example for all the ears that were listening.

In addition to changing the narrative around food and your self-talk, experiment with dinners. Save pasta night for when you eat out. Home is for protein, complex unprocessed carbs, and healthy fats. There are not good foods and bad foods, there is just food. In *The Washington Post* article titled, "There's no such thing as 'bad food.' Four terms that make dietitians cringe," the writer talks about the fact that broccoli can easily be considered a good food, but if that is all you eat all day long, it's not providing you with the essential nutrients you need to live. In that case, even "good food" becomes bad in effect

The analogy closer to home is that pizza is bad food. High in fat, refined carbs, and, well, you can easily eat a lot! However, if that pizza was served at a party the first night you moved into your new apartment and it brought your friends and neighbors together as they helped you unpack and settle in to create a home, it serves another purpose. It brought joy and belonging, and it nurtured your soul. You can picture everyone sitting around among the boxes laughing, can't you? All foods have a purpose, there is just a way to prioritize frequency and attitude and, in turn, appreciation. We must count food's nurturing effects as well as its nutritional value.

So no, don't talk to your kids about food and their weight. Model the behavior you want to see. Choose your words wisely about what you say when it comes to your own body. Take out the judgment when it comes to talking about food. Food is fuel. You wouldn't put water in a car and expect it to run. So, stop feeding your kids organic cheese snacks, protein bars, and fruit chews and then wonder why they are cranky and lethargic.

We Eat and Then We Move

Since your child knows how to ride a bike, get on one next to them and get moving. School-age children especially are sedentary most of the day. They may get 20 minutes outdoors for recess and possibly an hour for gym a few days a week. Otherwise, they are sitting at a desk.

If they are in an after school program, are they moving there? In a lot of cases, they aren't. And often they don't get to go outside. Some sort of movement practice should be a part of a child's life (and yours) each day. This could be a brisk walk, a dance session while dinner is cooking, or bike riding. Even organized activities like   tness classes, basketball, soccer, various team sports, gymnastics, and the like count. Remember these are not a replacement for the free play that is also essential for children—and even adults.

When given the option, choose to get somewhere by use of your own body versus by car, e-bike, e-scooter, or public transportation. Let the kids play at the playground every day once school is over or after their after-school program—in all weather. Remember, there is no such thing as bad weather, just bad clothing.

Prioritize movement. It doesn't have to be at a gym either. You can do at-home fitness challenges, just make them a must each day. Race your kid down the block every day before coming in for dinner or when they get home from school. Be sure to get your movement in before technology, TV watching, or other distractions happen and the day gets away from you. Incorporating a movement practice at a young age helps develop a habit for kids: that way, in the years to come, it's not something they have to add to their lives, especially at the bequest of a doctor. Life is coming fast, but it's important for all of us to slow down so we can get the shit that matters done.

If this shared movement practice challenges or intimidates you, acknowledge it and do it anyway. Your child and your own health need you to show up. Do your best, be consistent, and soon you will be looking at your own growth and how far you have come.

Wash Your Hands

So, we covered eating and moving. Now, onto another basic life skill: hygiene! It's time to cover everything from brushing your hair, brushing your teeth and flossing, bathing, clipping nails, changing clothes and bed sheets, washing hands after activities and before eating, to wiping your face after eating. A lot of these things are social norms too, and will help your child fit into society. Oh stop—I'm not asking you to make your child into a conformist—I'm asking that you teach your child to meet the base societal expectation when it comes to cleanliness and hygiene.

Will getting them to comply some days be harder than others? Yes! Will you give up the fight some days? Yes! Is this okay? Yes! Is tomorrow a new day? Yes! To be honest, I didn't brush my teeth in the morning (that I can remember) until I was in 7th grade. And if I didn't brush them in the morning, do you think I brushed them at night? Hell no. I didn't care. I don't remember if my parents fought me on it. I did go to the dentist every six months like clockwork. I didn't have a cavity until I was 18. In fact, to this day I have only had three cavities and I still have all my wisdom teeth. Well except the one that I knew I had trouble with and was told "Oh no, no, no. It's fine." And then crack—Tootsie Pop took it out one summer. It does only take three licks to get to the center of a Tootsie Pop—and apparently my tooth. But I digress.

I'm sure my parents picked their battles and this wasn't one of them. I learned on my own understanding through social and peer norms that I needed to be brushing my teeth! Trust me, it will work out. But, you need to have boundaries and expectations. If your child is adamant, let them out into the world and see how society deals with their feral roots. Maybe hearing whatever you're saying from someone else will make a difference.

Also, stop worrying about what other people think about your parenting. In the freezing weather, we pick up kids from school who don't have coats with them— just sweatshirts. During the hot afternoons, some kids have hoodies zipped all the way up. Kids are weird and do things that don't always make sense to us. You aren't a bad parent for letting your child make their own choices that seemingly may not be the best. They will learn. Let them express themselves. They are trying to see what fits. Don't swoop in and fix things for them. That kind of response creates a cycle of never-ending helplessness. You are not a bad parent for letting your child make choices and have some autonomy over their own lives.

Show Me the Money

Financial literacy is the new hot topic in life skills for kids. My parents were ahead of their time. When my brother and I were in elementary school, we had checkbooks my parents made for us to write checks in for things that we wanted. Obviously, we had tasks and things to do that earned us money in the bank.

Financial literacy is a fancy term for the ability to understand and use skills related to money such as learning financial management, creating and following a budget, and knowing how to grow your money over time (AKA investing). As someone who is financially literate, it means that you have a healthy relationship with money. You understand how money works and you're invested in a life-long journey of learning more about it and how it's meant to serve you as you live your journey. The earlier this happens in life, the easier it is to talk about money as kids grow into adults.

Specifically pertaining to kids, MYDOH, a financial app for parents and kids, owned by the Royal Bank of

Canada, says that the biggest part of financial literacy is understanding the essentials of how money works in our society since kids will earn it, save it, and protect it. MYDOH, meaning "my dough" AKA "my money," states that helping kids understand how to earn money and what they can do with it after they've earned it is one of the most important steps we can help them take as we encourage their journey toward greater financial literacy. I have never used this app and thus cannot speak to it specifically, but I'm down with their explanation.

As someone who spent a lot of their adult life in debilitating debt, the key takeaways I've discovered to leading a successful financial life are:

1. Live within your means
2. Pay yourself first.
3. Donate to someone or something else each pay period.

Suze Orman is a great fount of knowledge when it comes to getting out of debt as well as meeting your personal financial needs. But there is no one-size-fits-all money advice that works for everyone. For instance, I have life insurance, but I have no dependents, so I don't need life insurance. Now, at the time I got it, I was in my late twenties and thought I would need it. Life went in another direction. My financial advisor was smart enough to get me into a fund, so I have a cash value option if I choose to use the money myself. Otherwise, it's a simple gift that I'm leaving to my brother that makes me worth more in death than while I'm alive. Psst. DO NOT TELL HIM.

Suze teaches that we should put people first, next is money, and last is things. Keep that in mind when approaching this subject with your kids. I also like to put a value on experiences. Not all monetary investments need to show a physical object in return. Children are concrete learners and this will be a concept that might be somewhat difficult for them to grasp at first because it can be abstract.

When Disney's *Aladdin* first came out in the movie theater, I took one of my babysitting underlings out for a movie experience to celebrate his birthday. It was 1992! Danny, the birthday boy, must have been turning 5 or 6. I was a mere 19 years old. I took Danny and his older brother Brian to see the movie. We got popcorn and candy and probably soda—it was the '90s and kids drank soda. I spoiled them rotten and spent $50.00 of my hard-earned money. (Which would probably be $150.00 now!) Anyway, after taking them home, I said I hope you enjoyed the movie for your birthday. The little eyes looked up at me and said, "Chel, but where is my pwesent?" Little lisp and all. So, we had a conversation about the experience and spending time together being his present. Even then my love language was quality time, his not so much.

Let's look more deeply at the three takeaways for a successful financial life. You'll remember that the first one is always live within your means. That boils down to you spending less than you earn. You don't live off credit or take on costs that you can't afford so that you can compete with the Joneses. There were lean years when I had roommates in my railroad apartment. There was also a period of time when I moved back in with my parents in my thirties.

My Mom's rule was, "You can live here, but your stuff cannot—and no trips." The purpose of the move was to get my finances in order. My Mom was not about letting me live there essentially rent free *and* letting me jet set around the world at the same time. That's not how it was going to work. And so, it didn't.

I stopped using credit cards and made an aggressive weekly budget to pay down my debt.

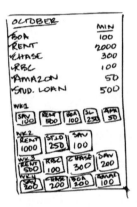

This plan was handwritten on a piece of paper with boxes and check marks. I didn't use fancy Excel spreadsheets at that point. Eventually though, I migrated to a spreadsheet my financial guru friend created that allowed me to manipulate the time and payments to sort out how much I would need to pay each month to get rid of my debt in however many months. I had another friend that used to pay her bills with money orders in the late 90s. As restaurant servers, we got paid primarily in cash. It worked best for her to take what she needed, pay her debts and then save the rest. The physical interaction with the money worked best for her. Even though I currently make enough money to pay my bills, I have one little trick up my sleeve. I don't spend my fives. Another friend told me about it. He started as a tribute to a fallen brother in the FDNY. What the original motivation was, I don't know, but this adds a little love to the story. After I collect my fives I usually end up with close to a $1000 in a year. I specifically use that money for FUN. To honor a fallen hero and to remind myself that it's important to enjoy life.

If you cannot pay your debts and current expenses on your salary, the best advice is to lower your expenses rather than try to make more money. I mean yes, start applying for jobs in the meantime. If your company doesn't see your value, even a lateral move to a new company can garner an increase in wages. That said, there is an immediate result when you lower your expenses, as you have complete control over a lot. Getting a raise is subject to so many outside circumstances.

For little kids, most of their expenses are going to be their wants, so the conversation will be more about saving than monthly expenses. And with that, we segue to paying yourself first.

The next key takeaway on the list is to pay yourself first. Yes, even if you have debt. You want to start building up an emergency fund in the event that you don't have a job, so you can continue to live your life without despair and worry. I used to set aside 10% of each paycheck in my savings account. Once that account reached $1,000.00, I would transfer it to an online savings account that I visually could only access by logging in to that account. It was pretty revolutionary for the time.

Now, there are high-yield interest-bearing accounts that pay upwards of 5%. Get in on that! Teach your child that their money can make money by not doing anything, which is called residual income. Now that's winning! Wait a minute, your kid doesn't get a paycheck and we aren't paying them for chores! Well, they will often get money for birthdays and milestones. Put the money out on the table and have them create three piles. Depending upon how old your child is, showing them in a concrete visible way will be much easier for them to understand.

Have them pay themselves first, then donate, and finally, create a "What I can spend now" stack. Explain to them that if there is something that they want that is more expensive than the spend now amount, they can put it into savings and keep a separate list of how much money they have saved. Money gifts too far and between? No problem. Add additional chores to your child's list that they can be paid for. These are separate from their family contribution chores and will not be paid if their family contribution chores are not completed. Stay strong, do not allow them to cherry pick!

Now, you can start having conversations about the value of work. If their efforts do not match what they are capable of, have a conversation about expectations, pride, and integrity. Doing the bare minimum is not enough. Instill in them a great work ethic now. Explain that we do this for ourselves, not to necessarily be recognized and rewarded by others, but that this merit will be proof positive of the next step in a career, a raise, or a promotion. And if doesn't, it's proof positive why you deserve them and are pursuing another job to go where you are valued.

The last takeaway is to donate some of the money. I'm not saying to tithe your money: I'm saying donate to a cause that is near and dear to your heart. Put it on auto pay each month. It can even be a small amount—whatever is within your means. When you give, you make room to receive.

My monthly donations started at $20.00 each. Then, as I made more money, I increased to $50.00 and so on. It is not money that I miss. So, choose an amount that works for you, even if it's $5.00 per month.

My donations are to organizations that match my core values, equity and love, and the groups that I champion, women and children. It's okay to change it up after a while too. Don't forget, you can also set things up to give a gift from your estate in the future: just make the company a beneficiary even if it's 5-10%

When thinking of how you want to donate, ask your child what is important to them. It could be that they value the environment, or that their school chums have food to eat, or that there are toys for kids to play with. It's okay to have conversations about children that don't have everything they want or need or live in foster care and might need help from others. Most children have no idea that other kids out there have lives that are so drastically di erent from theirs. The awareness and practice of donating teaches empathy. Later, we'll talk about donating our time, but for now, let's stick to the money.

At our camps, the kids decided to make bracelets to sell. You know the rubber ones where all the loose parts end up everywhere, including in your vacuum? Yeah, those. The opportunity organically presented itself, so we had a conversation about expenses, labor, and profits. I fronted supply costs for the first round as those supplies were already at the gym. For the second round, they paid me for the goods (wholesale because I'm nice). They determined a fair wage for everyone that was involved and out of the profits, they donated a certain percentage to the local organization that we volunteered with on a weekly basis.

Ironically, the director of that organization's own son yucked on our yum by saying the donation wasn't a lot. Trust me when I say that his mother, the director, put him in his place. Our kids and hers learned a valuable lesson that day. The donations kept coming in through the remainder of the summer and it was such a wonderful learning experience for the kids. I found out a few weeks ago that some of the older kids had started a company soon after and applied the financial principles that we taught them that summer to running something on their own. It was so amazing to hear that those lessons stuck and that the campers understood the importance of what they learned during camp. There are ways to do this at any level as long as you meet your child where they are right now.

Kind to be Kind (Cruelty Has No Place Here)

Is choosing kindness really a life skill? These days I would say "Yes." At the gym, we pride ourselves on connecting with our families and giving them a quality of service and care above our competition. We often get comments and looks of surprise at how much we invest in our relationships.

We don't necessarily think we are doing anything above and beyond, I mean we are talking about children here. The truth of the matter, though, is that automation and technology continue to replace the interactions we make a point to create with our gym kids. So, when people get individualized attention, they are sometimes blown away. I heard once that these days kindness is often being misinterpreted as flirting. To me, that tells us that almost no one is really choosing kindness enough.

So, what about teaching kindness to our kids? Are we modeling kind behavior for them? To me, kindness includes basic manners like saying "hello" and "goodbye," or a courtesy like holding the door or greeting people you have interactions with—things that the barista or grocery cashier are expected to do as part of their jobs. They deserve our grace too.

Kindness also means walking on the proper side of the sidewalk and leaving space for others, saying "Excuse me" when needed, apologizing when appropriate (not gratuitously out of default because of people-pleasing tendencies), and, of course, sharing with others what they mean to us for no reason. Kids especially probably don't hear from adults other than their parents about the joy and love they bring to the lives of others. So, don't be afraid to tell them. And with those ideas as the foundation for what kindness looks like, let's get more specific, shall we

Examples of how we teach kindness at Gantry Kids:

At the gym, when I'm there, the kids come in and some say hello. In a playful way, I'll remind the kids who don't greet me that they just came in my house and need to say hello. We've mentored our coaches to include kids in the politeness conversation so they know their role.

For instance, saying "Please" and "Thank You" together after a request seems commonplace these days. Not at the gym. The kids need to be a part of the exchange and conversation. Saying "Please" and "Thank You" together tells them that they have no part in the niceties, but also in what is asked of them. By saying both parts of what should be a multi-part interaction all at the beginning of that interaction, we're taking away the actual meaning of the words and instead making them a thoughtless habit. The entire dialogue came and went and frankly, they probably didn't register a thing, including what you asked them to do. Save the thanks for after the task is done.

We also ask that children answer questions when we speak to them. If a child just stares at you when you talk to them or ask a question, this is a teaching moment to give that child their voice. We tell them "If you don't know the answer, it's okay to say 'I don't know.'" You can also instruct them that "If you don't want to talk to me, just say, 'Hi, I'm doing something right now and I don't want to talk.'"

Regarding kindness and respect toward others, we don't tolerate it when children are unkind to one another or our coaches. However, we also don't believe in zero-tolerance policies. If we go back to Piaget's cognitive development chart and Erikson's psychosocial stages, they remind us that children are learning. Kids don't transfer knowledge until a much older age and this means we can't expect them to get things right on the first try

So, sometimes it looks like they are being unkind when they just don't know that their actions have an impact. Now, as much as we think that children deserve a safe space to grow and learn, we are in communication with parents about the different interactions that take place between their children and others. Physical or verbal aggressions are still expressions. Whether they are displays of frustration or the inability to articulate emotions, these responses are still related to feelings that are real.

For example, if your child continually starts fights, we are going to speak to you. If your child continually antagonizes others verbally and ends up getting pushed or shoved, we talk to the parents of both parties. Physical aggression doesn't trump verbal aggression when it comes to the blame game.

Our rule is that it is never okay to start things, but it is okay to defend yourself—if that means a shove or a push, so be it. No, I'm not encouraging violence of any kind, but if a child is taunting and teasing your child and they defend themselves by telling the other kid to shut their pie hole or by pushing the other kid out of their face, I'm okay with that for young elementary age kids. Check out the charts again. Are you expecting your child to respond in a way that they aren't capable of simply because of where they are in the stages of development?

Your child stood up for themselves, was in control of their life, and handled things. The other child got what they deserved and will probably think twice about their next move. I also want to be clear and say that this is not a conversation about repeated bullying, either. That conversation would go differently. Remember kids are going to get into things sometimes, and with our guidance, they can come out the other side of the conflict successfully. Again, this is where the magic happens.

The greatest way to practice kindness is to give your child their voice. Encourage them to have interactions with people outside their family, like the server at the restaurant, or the person behind you leaving the store. This is practice that will serve them well as they grow into adults.

CHAPTER 9

Talking About the Hard Stuff

It seems to be a trend these days that parents are referring to their children as their best friends. That sounds so sweet, and yes you love them that much, *but* you are also their parent. Being your child's best friend will come later in life, when your role has shifted to advisor and touchstone versus teacher and guardian of safety. It will all come full circle.

A child in the developmental years needs boundaries to feel safe. And, they need someone who is in charge of the situation we call life. If you are more their friend than their parent, they often end up in the driver's seat and choose what feels good versus what is necessary. Remember failed gentle parenting? This includes successfully passing through Piaget's developmental stages and Erikson's psychosocial stages.

Remember that conflict is where we learn. So, stay grounded and committed to who you are to your child and what your true role is in their upbringing: You are their parent. There is a place inside of that for love, tenderness, and eventually being their best friend.

Being their parent means you need to acknowledge your child's feelings while also having boundaries and guidelines about appropriate behavior. If there are no boundaries, a child will use their feelings and how those feelings impact you to manipulate situations to get what they want. I've seen it a million times and I've had it done to me too. When you know to watch out for this, you will start to see patterns.

A great example of this kind of behavior happened during the pandemic when we were basically running a school at the gym. A kindergartener's behavior fell short of our expectations. I can't even remember what it was, nothing of significance, but enough that it needed to be addressed. I am a very fair and even person, but I will not mince words: I take the time to explain social interactions to children so they can understand that their actions and words have an impact and matter.

So, as I was calmly discussing the issues with the child, their eyes started to well up and they started crying. I was very empathetic and asked why they were crying and stated, "How I feel about you hasn't changed. I still love you and am so glad you are here. I did not like your behavior and I'd like for you to share what you can do differently next time." The tears subsided and we continued on.

The next few times something happened, the tears would flow fast. Each time, I was a little sterner in the discussion and said that they need to use their words and crying wasn't going to fix anything (or something like that). Listen, I was kind and empathetic, but also called them out on their strategies. There are some kids that are always crying, or always being dicks, and it's not because they are afraid or don't know any better: It's because those tactics have gotten them what they wanted before.

Adults, we are being manipulated. Yes, it's true. A child may not know it's manipulation, but they know, "this is how I get what I want." Learning this behavior is part of growing up, but so is learning to put a stop to it. There are patterns that are visible if you take a look. Notice also that I got real after a few times, when I was able to identify the pattern with certainty. I remember like it was yesterday being at the bottom of the stairs crying after a nightmare or something. My Dad came up from our basement rec room and was so sweet. He then carried me upstairs. The next night, no nightmare in sight, I tried again. My Dad came up and just gave me a look and said "We aren't doing this," and sent me on my way. You really do turn into your parents as you get older.

After that last exchange, the child stopped crying when he was "in trouble" and we saw so much growth in him. He grew up a little in that moment because I took the time to have an honest conversation where I shared what I saw and offered another solution than their default method to cope with issues. Be that person for your child. Become a love diplomat, if you will! The best way to start is to set clear boundaries for your relationship.

Manners is another vital piece of kindness to teach kids, as we discussed in our life skills section. First, teach them the habits of saying "please" and "thank you." Next, instruct them to address a person when that person walks into a room. Then, explain to them that they should call their parents by "Mom" and "Dad" instead of "she" and "him." Did you notice I capitalized mom and dad anytime I'm referring to mine? Although grammatically incorrect, it's something I do to honor and respect them. Finally, teach them to address elders with some formality and respect like "Ms. Michele" or "Coach Deanna" etc. Like I mentioned earlier, whenever the kids come into the gym, I tell them,

"Hey, you just came into my house, say hello to me!" I'm sure half of them think I live there!

I also mentioned previously that we work with kids to answer questions from adults too. Why? Because I have received so many blank stares. When a child doesn't answer my question, the first thing I do is check that they heard me. Then, I ask if they understood what I asked. Next, I ask why they didn't answer me. Finally, I explain when they don't answer me that I think:

1. There is something wrong and that's why they didn't answer. My question at that point is, "Did something happen that upset you?"

2. They are choosing to be rude instead of choosing to be kind. It is rude not to answer someone when they ask you a question. In a community, we use our words to talk and connect with one another. When you ignore someone it can be hurtful to them.

I also give them permission to say, "I didn't hear you," "I don't understand," "I don't know," or "Hey I'm not in the mood to talk today."

A while ago, I was at a friend's party and her 4-year-old, who normally chats it up with me, totally blew me o . Later on in the day, I said to him, "Hey how come you aren't talking to me?" He said, "Because I want to be with my friends. I don't want to talk to you." I said, "Okay, that's cool. Do you think saying hi to me and saying you're going to see your friends would take a long time?" He said "No."

At that point, I explained that I thought maybe he was mad at me and that's why he didn't answer me. He said, "No, I'm not!" but with such a look of bewilderment on his face. It was as if, until that moment, he thought it was impossible for him to impact someone else. I said, "Well,

I'm glad you're not upset, and next time just say 'Hi,' and "See ya later, I'm hanging with my friends today.'" He said, "Okay." And the next time I saw him—voila! Hi and bye and going to hang with my friends. There was a benefit for him in the initial exchange as well. Communicating effectively and directly just feels good. Plus, knowing you did right by someone gives you a sense of accomplishment and belonging in the community. It's a success in the enterprise versus inability phase!

While we are on the subject, I don't force children to hug or kiss or fist bump or anything. Before basic consent became a conversation, I always asked children if I could have a hug, and sometimes they would (and still do) say "No," which is fine. I never liked being forced to hug and kiss adults, especially the friends of my parents who only came around a few times a year—or the ones that smoked a thousand cigarettes: peeyouu. It feels awkward when physical interaction is forced.

With that being said, it is not a lot to ask a child to acknowledge another human being with a verbal hello. It teaches manners, respect, and builds confidence—all while reducing their potential future anxiety of being in groups where they don't know how to act. In my humble opinion, I think a lot of anxiety starts because we don't put ourselves in situations where we actually have to manage being uncomfortable often enough. And parents are extending that to their kids.

It's one thing if we need to face situations where we rarely find ourselves, like jumping out of a plane or fl ing 10+ hours. But when we avoid situations that come up a lot, like going somewhere alone—whether it's to meet someone or to attend an event where we won't know anyone—it's often easier to avoid the situation than work through the anxiety.

Also, the way to work through anxiety is by physically changing your body, not your mind. So breathing, exercise, and movement are needed instead of putting yourself through mental gymnastics by trying to be more logical. Please be careful when describing your child or yourself as having anxiety. It is perfectly normal and okay to have butterflies, mild sweats, or heart flutters in certain situations. It means you are alive!

Avoiding the situations that cause these physical responses is not the right answer. Acknowledge that uncomfortable feeling, take deep breaths, and then go after the thing you want or need to do. There are people in the world who really do suffer from extreme anxiety and who need medication and therapy to face the world daily. There is no logic or reason in their game. Self-proclaimed anxiety takes away from the severity of their experience. Tread lightly is all I'm saying.

Teach your kids the basics: They need to speak to people and make eye contact. Practice with family and then start having them do it out in the world while you are still by their side. They need to order their own ice cream, be the one to pay for items at the store and wait for the change. And they need to ask for themselves whether it is okay with an owner if they pet the owner's dog (please always ask). And if your child doesn't want to be the one to ask for ice cream, then just explain, "Well, I can't ask for you, I have to order my own and you need to do the same." Or if they don't want to talk to the dog owner, you can say, "I don't want to pet the dog, but you do, so you should be the one to ask." Make sure to read the room, though. If they are super scared, then start the convo, "Hi, my child has a question," and prompt your child to take over. It's okay if they walk away without petting the dog because they didn't want to ask. It might help them gain the courage for the next time, because they know they missed an opportunity.

Now, that doesn't seem like such hard stuff, does it? The reason for having a child engage in the world is that it gives them an idea of what social norms are: specifically what is conventional behavior and what could be deemed as threatening behavior.

Take stranger danger out of your vocabulary and start using strange behavior as an indicator now that your child has been speaking to and making eye contact with various people, friends, family, and strangers. One stranger or family member always stands a little too close or is physically too a ectionate toward them. Like touching their neck or patting their back. This is a time to discuss how this makes your child feel and what to do about it. A stranger talking to them at a food truck is not a red flag

Check in with them by asking questions like, "I saw that you ran away after Uncle Buck was talking to you. Was everything okay?" If they reply, "Yes, he just smelled like cigarettes and I didn't like it since he always stands so close to me" then acknowledge that they had a good solution by keeping the interaction short. If they answered, "No, I always feel weird with Uncle Buck. He holds my hand too long, and always says weird things, but I don't really remember them." You can continue to ask open-ended questions about how that person makes them feel, their fears about that person's related actions, and then talk about what they could do. Every child needs to listen to their inner compass.

Children know what is right and wrong and we need to acknowledge that. Also, give them permission to say something to the offending party. A child that tells an adult that their behavior is weird to them and they don't like it can actually stop an adult from continuing the behavior. If an adult chooses to keep doing it, then it is your place as the parent to say something to them. Adults that dismiss children are a threat to that child for a number of reasons, which could be anything from intentions to groom that child, or blatant disregard for that child's autonomy. This includes when we, their parents, poo-poo their concerns. The impact of those behaviors creates varying degrees of trauma for the involved child.

I had an uncle that said weird stuff to me. Like at my high school graduation, he commented on my weight. I just looked at him, said "Thanks so much." In my best Jersey Girl sassy way, and walked in the opposite direction. I had never had a true relationship with him or given his words any value in my life. Even still, I felt weird about it. So, I told my Mom at that moment, and I'm sure she ripped him a new one. The look she gave me in that moment and the "I'll handle it" as she was elbows deep in food prep, made me feel protected and safe.

Sometimes all a kid can do is confide in an adult. That is the place for us to help them solve the problem. With that being said, it's much easier when dealing with unwanted conversations and even hurtful words to have a response already set up. Then it is something the child just goes for and doesn't have to think about in that moment. "That's not very nice, don't talk to me that way," is a good one, then they take a turn on their heels and go.

As an adult, I'm still caught off guard sometimes, like when I had surgery and the anesthesiologist made some weird date-rapey comment in regards to the level of anesthesia I might need. It was completely inappropriate, and that happened in 2023. My response was "Is that how you had to meet your wife?" I shared with the doctor at my follow-up what happened because not everyone has a quick snarky response time like mine. Plus, the level of care I got from the doctor didn't match what happened that day. She needed to know. Just because I handled it doesn't mean I wasn't disappointed or tired from the interaction. It felt like, "Here we go again, even in a place where I need to feel safe, I'm getting harassed."

I had a 7-year-old girl at the gym come up to me once and say, "This person did this to me." On cue, I said "And what did you say back?" She said, "I told him, that was not very nice, and don't do that again. And if he keeps doing it, no one will want to be his friend." I looked that 7-year-old square in the face and said, "Well it sounds like you handled it. Good work. Is there anything you need from me?" She said, "No," and skipped on her way.

I will never forget how visible her true self was to me that day. No tears, just the what's so. No drama, just the what's so. Get it girl! And just because she handled it doesn't mean she wasn't hurt or impacted by the interaction. But, she still acted in way that allowed her to communicate what she wasn't okay with. So, offer your support in these types of situations. "Is there anything I can do?" is a great place to start.

The more exposure children have to interactions whether with a peer or an adult, the more nuanced their understanding will be on what strange behavior looks like versus just a stranger. The more conversations you have with your child about different interactions, the more clarity they will have about how to manage things: and they will also feel safe and supported by you, their parent. This process also helps kids learn to trust their guts and be led by their inner compasses. Once they build this skill, it becomes more and more clear when they are taken off the path of their true north.

Navigating the Not-So-Nice

We've touched upon di cult things in previous chapters, but I want to take a few minutes to go into greater detail about the not-so-nice stu . Life can be scary. There are predators out there and also not-so-nice people: But, really most people are inherently good.

Remember that often it is tempting to make decisions based on our fears—and many of our fears are based on negligible statistics. This should logically make a difference, but when it comes to matters of love and protection, it's a little harder to make our brains agree. Am I right? So, how do you encourage your child to be independent when you are afraid that darkness might lurk on every corner? You do your best. Part of doing your best is having hard conversations with your kids so they know what to do and how to navigate life. You can start by laying out basic practices to help with safety and to assuage *your* fears.

Safety in Numbers

As your child is getting older and asserting more independence, let them know there is safety in numbers. This is true whether they are walking home from school with a group of friends, or choosing a subway car with more than two people in it. Explain that there are bad people out there and some do want to harm others, but statistically, there's almost a zero percent chance of that happening. Explain to them that it's important for you to have that conversation with each other so they don't feel scared or worried. A good tip is to have them always stay both in a group and in the public eye.

Be Present

Help your child understand that when they are walking down the street, it is important to put their phones and headphones away so they can pay attention to where they are going and what is going on around them. People who are distracted make ideal targets.

Criminals want simple, easy targets. If your kid is looking down at their phone or blaring music through their headphones, they are an easy target—of theft or worse. Also, help them understand that they don't need to be bogged down with so many bags and items that they can barely navigate walking around. That would also make them an easy target. So, teach them to be present! And lead by example.

Be Loud & Proud

Loudness or audibility in a person tells the rest of the world that they are there, and seen! I'm not saying kids should scream and yell as they cavort around with their friends, but the day of children being seen and not heard is over.

Teach them to let the world know that they exist, that they know their own voice, and that they belong there. I'm so loud that when people ask how tall I am and I say 5'5" they scoff and say "No, you're taller." I simply reply, "No, that's my personality."

Fight Like Hell

In the event that something strange or bad does happen, tell your child it's okay to fight like hell. I've had too many conversations with kids where they say that they feel bad about hurting someone while trying to get away. My response is straightforward and I tell them, "If they are trying to hurt you, your job is to fight like hell and not care how they feel."

Now, I'm not going to do a deep dive on when it's appropriate to do as you're told or to fight like hell. Why? Frankly, if someone is holding a gun to my head trying to get me in a car, I'm going to fight like hell. If they are holding a knife and just want my phone and wallet, I might give it to them. If and when that next to zero percent statistic of kidnapping by a stranger happens, your child should fight like hell.

Also, note that you can't truly practice self-defense, so don't think showing your kids some moves is going to help. It might hurt more because your child isn't willing to do what is absolutely necessary to get out of your hold if you practice with them. They may walk away thinking they aren't strong enough or actually able to get away from anyone. Teach them to kick, bite, knee privates, bend back fingers, and do anything else that will help them get free. The goal is to have them feel confident and capable after your conversations. Oh, and sport martial arts are also not self-defense: send them for the activity, not life training.

Other Not-So-Nice Topics

Although this one is not as difficul as conversations about kidnapping and bodily harm, talk to your kids about what to do if they get lost or separated from you. As you already read, our plan at the gym if a child ends up apart from the group—on the subway, any public transportation, at a museum, or while we are biking—is to stay still. They know to wait for us. We will come back. They also know to let an aiding adult or police office know what our plan is and that this adult can wait with them in that spot.

See, if they move, we won't know where they went. If we retrace our steps, we will find them fast. Setting kids up with a plan of what to do in the event that something scary happens gives them confidence and practical steps to execute the fix. We walk through these steps with them mentally: Imagine being separated from the group, not knowing what to do, and being offered help by a stranger that says let's go somewhere else. Why? Because, how can anyone make a decision inside of such fright if they aren't mentally prepared?

Knowledge is power: give it to your children. Oh, and let your kids know what your family plan is for when you are with the family and a separation occurs. Camp, school, and other places may have their own plan and they should follow that speci c plan when they are there. Feel free to adopt our strategies!

Conversations That Matter

Bringing up hard things will not make your child afraid or put a blemish on either their free spirit or childhood. Bets are that they are already hearing things from other kids and your conversations will ease their concerns. Don't be afraid: You can do the hard things too.

CHAPTER 10

Being of Service

When I think of important life skills, being of service to others is pretty high on my list. It is so important to teach children how to think about and act in care for others. When we are of service to our fellow humans, we learn selflessness, empathy, gratitude, and community—and also that we live in a great big world. Being of service can look differently depending on each person's passion.

For example, your kid might love volunteering at a soup kitchen, packing lifeline grocery boxes, painting a community mural, volunteering at a community function, or baking cookies for the school bake sale. They might also enjoy mowing a neighbor's lawn, helping clean up after a big storm, building houses for Habitat for Humanity, donating money they've gotten as a gift to a charity, or having a lemonade stand and donating the proceeds to a favorite charity. It can look any way they want.

An Amazing Example

It is also awesome if your kids see you modeling this behavior. Growing up, my parents were always being of service. My Mom made sandwiches for volunteers at Habitat for Humanity. She said she couldn't build the house, so she would feed the people swinging hammers. As a family, we volunteered at a soup kitchen a few times a year. We always took a giving ornament from both our church's giving tree and the one at the local bookstore.

Then, on my own as a young adult, I was a big with Big Brothers Big Sisters and helped paint the hallways of underserved schools. Now, the gym donates monthly in honor of both my parents. I remember as a child realizing that not everyone had it as good as me. Even children are impacted by food insecurity and poverty, and if it's not us making a difference, then who's it going to be?

I'm sharing this with you as an exercise on how to be of service. It's not to toot my own horn or get accolades. My parents were against eulogies for themselves. I vetoed my Dad at my Mom's funeral because I just felt a need for the world to know her value and what an exceptional human being she was. And not just to me, but also to others: she did it all selflessly. When my Mom died, she left a hole in the world that needed to be filled. Ordinary people often do extraordinary things.

Years later, as I've gotten older, I understand why they didn't want eulogies. My parents did things to contribute, make a difference for others, and add more love to the world. But they didn't live their lives for recognition. The same thing goes for being of service. You don't need to hide your contribution, but remember to teach your child the heart of the matter: being of service to others is not about them.

Getting the Kids Involved

Early on in our camps, I was taking a group through the city on foot near Madison Square Park. They saw a youngish man poking through the trash. There were definitely a few ews that came from the group of 7- and 8-year-olds. They seemed confused about why anyone would eat out of the trash. I said to them, "He doesn't have food or money and that's where he can find some food." One child (who at the writing of this book is now in college, mind you) said, "But still." I then explained, "If he doesn't eat out of the trash, he isn't going to eat at all."

The 8-year-old looked right at me and said only, "Oh." It had not occurred to him that someone would rifle through the trash out of necessity, not having a home to return to for a proper meal, as if the rummaging was simply because they wanted an afternoon snack. I was determined not to end the conversation there. Next, I asked what we could do rather than judge. Some said we could buy him food. Others said we could give him money. I agreed and said, "We can also show him some respect and grace for doing what he needs to do." Which means checking our own attitudes and what we say both in our heads and aloud to others.

After that, we began incorporating being of service as one of the pillars of summer camp. Over the years, we have packed grocery boxes for people experiencing food insecurity and sold both lemonade and friendship bracelets to raise money for different organizations. One year, we helped paint a mural in our community to beautify the area.

Each new academic year, we have conversations about community and why it's important to contribute to others that may need a little help. The younger kids may not have a complete understanding of their reach, but they get to be a part of something bigger than themselves and they learn to give with the expectation of receiving nothing in return. As the kids get older, they understand the importance of providing for others, especially because they get that kids their own age are in the mix of people in need.

What's In It for Me?

Anytime a child does anything these days—whether helping with or participating in some activity or event—they always ask "Well, what do I get?" Often times my answer is "The satisfaction of knowing you did a good job." Insert crying laughing emoji.

When we lay out the expectations of being of service— that there is no reward—the kids still walk away with something. Whether it is the satisfaction in the work that they did or the knowledge that what they did made a difference for someone else, it's a win. Plus, they learn something of value. I mean, in *Friends*, Joey and Phoebe debate whether a selfless act truly does exist: I'd have to say no. Not only does more come to you as you give, but you also get a sense of peace and pride in the contribution you have become to the world around you. Whenever I'm wallowing in my own self-pity, I set a timer. When the time is up, I step outside of myself and do something for someone else. Being of service to others has restorative properties.

Being of service also teaches people empathy and grace. We help because we can and we get the added surprise bonus of potentially walking in another person's shoes: or at least standing near that person. If we're given the opportunity to interact with the families benefiting from our work, we learn that we aren't that different from them. Sometimes it's luck or fate that separates us from one another. Children, especially, are in such situations because of the actions of adults. They are experiencing the circumstances, not causing or contributing to them.

Allowing your child to befriend and interact with their peers from a different walk of life tells your child and their friend that we are all on the same journey in the universe. There may even be a school chum of your child's that needs a friend and who your child will reach out to after they have an experience that's prompted by being of service.

Without you having to point out that they should feel gratitude, children will automatically experience thankfulness as a direct result of being of service to others. Once you explain where you are going, what you are doing, and describe the people who need help, your little will begin to see the riches in their own life.

Children have gone home from our camps and chosen toys to donate to organizations or asked their parents if they could do something to help someone else as a family. Simply put, kids learn by being exposed to life. When you incorporate being of service into their lives at such a young age, you're providing many valuable lessons as well as engaging kids in the practice of empathy and understanding. And all of these opportunities—ones that you provide for your kids—lead to more kindness in the world.

CHAPTER 11

Snitches Get Stitches

I got your attention, didn't I? Well, now that you're riveted, this chapter is about behaviors, but mostly for parents. We've gotten to a point in time where adults' words and concepts are being applied to child behavior. Kindergarteners are being taken out of school in handcuffs and parents are threatening lawsuits where there is just no place for them.

The two issues I come across most are bullying and assault. Actually, what I mean to say is that I most often come across the misuse of the terms bullying and assault by both parents and children.

Is It Actually Bullying?

The definition I found that I think really adequately describes bullying is from The National Centre Against Bullying (NSAB). They are an Australian organization dedicated to fighting bullying and keeping children safe.

The way the NSAB defines bullying is by clarifying that it is an ongoing and intentional use of power in relationships through consistent spoken, physical, and group behavior.

The biggest requirement is that that it's rooted in causing psychological harm to one person or to a group of people. In addition, the NSAB adds that in bullying, a group or individual misapplies their power, or power that is sensed, to an individual or group of people who feel that they can't stop or prevent the actions related to that abuse of power.

Bullying doesn't have to take place in a physical space. It can happen to someone both in person and online. There are di erent platforms where bullying takes place, and it can be obvious or hidden from the public view. One of the important things to think about when determining if bullying has occurred is whether the behavior has happened repeatedly or could be repeated over time.

In addition to those things, at the root of all bullying, is the intent to cause harm. It can have impact on the right now even after a few instances, and it can also have long-term effects for those who are bullied or who experience others being bullied.

With all that in mind, the NSAB goes one step further to discuss what is *not* bullying. They explain that one-o instances, conflicts, or fights between two people who have equal power—whether it's happening in a physical or digital space—should not be identified as bullying.

The NSAB also goes further to say that social rejection, dislike, spite-related single episode acts, moments of random aggression, single episodes of intimidation, and general arguments or disagreements are social interactions that do not qualify as bullying. They explain, though, that these actions do cause intense distress, but are *not* bullying because of the missing deliberate and repeated actions.[26]

26 National Center Against Bullying, "Definition of Bullying: National Centre Against Bullying," National Center Against Bullying, accessed August 29, 2023, https://www.ncab.org.au/bullying-advice/bullying-for-parents/definition-of-bullying/.

Please re-read the last two paragraphs to see what bullying is *not*. Even the definition of bullying includes an intent to cause harm. A child needs to intend to hurt another, whether physically or psychologically, for it to be bullying. Conflict happens. Aggression happens. Disagreements happen. Kids get made fun of. That doesn't mean that your child is being bullied.

I will be the one to say this because some aren't willing to: if someone is being unkind, a dick, or hurtful toward your child, then your child needs to say something to that person directly. They need to tell them to knock it o and it's not very nice, just like that badass 7-year-old girl I mentioned earlier did.

Did you know that legally, if we are being harassed by someone, we have a duty to tell them to stop. If you do not tell them to stop, there isn't a lot the legal system can do for you. Despite it being seemingly obvious that we don't want to be spoken to or treated in a particular way, we have a duty to let the other person know. We must assert that the behavior is unwanted and to put the aggressor on notice. Then, if they continue, we have standing to pursue some sort of claim or restitution. If we aren't going to say anything, how can we expect there to be change? That's everywhere in life, right?

Now, at the gym we do our best to keep tabs on what is happening between kids, just like every other facility and school does. But, we can't see or know everything. So, if your child comes to you and says someone is bullying them, before you come to me or someone on my staff, please ask your child the following questions: What happened? Where did it happen? How often has it happened? Did you say anything to them before? Did you say anything to them after? Did you tell a teacher or coach? Find out everything. These questions are open and will help you avoid guiding your child to agree with a story you are telling. As hard as it is, keep to the facts.

Validate your child's feelings by having a discussion with them about what there is to do. Coach them to confront the aggressor. Give them a voice to stand up for themselves. You calling me or any other caregiver and demanding I do something about it isn't going to help your child. Should you call me? Yes, of course. We are partners. So, let's make sure to partner. Support your child in taking care of themselves and contact me so that I can do the same. We will talk to the other child, of course—but your kid needs to know how to take care of themselves too. You can't fight all their battles for them.

In situations that involve conflict, be on alert. Remember that section where I talked about manipulation? Kids are smart. They know bullying is not tolerated, and they probably think it's synonymous with being annoying and hurtful. The word "bullying" is the soup du jour of buzz words that kids know will get our attention. Calling someone a bully now gets a gasp in the crowd response, and a branding, or scarlet letter affixed to the perpetrator's shirt. Kids know it's power, even if you don't know the complexities and long-lasting effect of labeling a peer as such.

I was an incredibly sensitive child and I became upset if the wind blew the wrong way. I've been an empath, but I was also impacted deeply by outside circumstances. As we know, my Dad used to say to me, "No one can make you feel a particular way, only you can do that." Now, in the thick of it back then, I would sob and say "Nooooo that's not true, they did this to meeeeeeee." I didn't understand that I could control my emotional reactions.

Even though Sally was mean to me, I allowed that to impact me in such a deep-rooted way. My Dad's words were also not the same as "Don't let it bother you." That's just denying how you feel, which doesn't actually help. My Dad gave me the power to choose how I could feel. It's a difficul exercise, but worth the practice, especially for young people.

When you choose how to respond to your emotions as a child or teen, you grow up recognizing that people's actions aren't always about you, that they are doing their best, and being a dick to you is sometimes the best that they have in them. I'm not saying we need to accept that behavior. I'm just saying that there is power in knowing their actions are not a reflection of you or have any power over you!

I had a woman come up to me after an interaction with her husband at an airport lounge. He had cut the line and I was seemingly annoyed. In fairness, he didn't realize he had cut the line. She said to me, "I don't want this to ruin your day." As much as I objected, there was truth in what she said. The di erence between adult me and kid me is that I fully knew that I would be choosing to have that man, that interaction, ruin my day by keeping that moment alive each time I chose to retell the story. Guess what? I didn't retell the story once after I walked away, recognizing my own power. Let's give kids that same opportunity. What if you had had that opportunity as a young person? How much teenage angst would have dissolved before it really got going?

Now, are there instances where kids are getting bullied? Sure. To be honest, with the little kids, it's because they are vulnerable which makes them easy targets. I'm not saying that they are doing anything to bring the bullying on—they are just low-hanging fruit. Because of that, the minute they come back at the aggressor, it usually shuts the aggressor down. This means that not everything needs to be managed by an adult.

Kids need to learn to take care of themselves and not rely on us for every little thing. If they take action on their own, they will learn what self-respect is as well as peer respect. Anyway, the point is that yes, kids are getting bullied out there. Is it likely that your child who attended our camp for two days is being bullied because kids made fun of his scooter? Probably not according to the definition we discussed. Is it still hurtful? Yes. But, can we control how we feel? Also yes.

Is It Actually Assault?

Another favorite I've run into with parents is the word assault. It has been used on a few occasions to describe behaviors at the camp or the gym. Assault. Yes, you read that correctly. Cornell Law explains that legally, assault must be intentional in manner and put an intended person (or persons) in understandable worry of looming harm or objectionable contact.[27]

This means that your child is reasonably apprehensive about the situation (not you, your child). So, if your child is in some sort of physical conflict with another child and repeatedly goes back to play with them, that is not assault because they clearly are not apprehensive. Can these situations turn into instances of manipulation and abuse? Yes, but until a child is apprehensive, scared, or even worried and confused, this isn't it.

---

27   Cornell Law School, "Intentional Tort," Legal Information Institute, accessed August 29, 2023, https://www.law.cornell.edu/category/keywords/intentional_tort/.

Did you also know that the penal law in New York State (and most other states) requires that the assault involved a direct intent to harm another? So, the aggressor has to want to hurt the other person and they actually have to have caused such harm. I feel like this is a good place to remind you that I went to law school, which is why I think about these concepts from what I find to be a usefully precise perspective.

You know the other thing that is so important is that up until recently, children 7 years of age and younger were not considered capable of committing a crime in the state of New York. They did not have the *mens rea*, or state of mind, to actually commit a crime. The Raise the Age Bill was signed into effect beginning October 1st, 2018 for 16-year-olds and October 1st, 2019 for 17-year-olds in New York State and raised the age of criminal responsibility to 18 years old.[28] So, a child cannot commit a crime before the age of 18. It's not a free pass: in most cases, criminal activity done by a child under 18 is referred to social services and family court. The circumstances and severity of the crime determine where the case is adjudicated.

My point is, assault doesn't exist for children under the age of 7 and for children up to age 18 it needs to fit the definition. I had a parent call us because her child was "being assaulted by another child". I responded that they are calling each other besties and I cannot keep your child away from her, despite having conversations about it—so, in fact, there is no assault.

---

28   New York State Government, "Raise the Age," The State of New York, accessed August 29, 2023, https://www.ny.gov/programs/raise-age-0.

In another instance, a bottle of hand sanitizer was opened and burped up into two kids' faces. Again, it wasn't assault. Actually, it was just an accident. No one was hurt, maybe just a little startled. But please keep emailing me your outlandish accusations. Also, don't email me. If you are that concerned with behaviors, call me. Things can be sorted out much faster and friendlier over a call. As a lawyer, I'm happy to write up a synopsis of the conversation afterward. This brings me to my next point.

Please ask more questions. I tell our coaches that children are to be believed and listened to, and their job is to find the truth by asking questions. Even when you think you've heard it all, there is always another question to be asked. The general *they* says there are three sides to every story: yours, mine, and the truth.

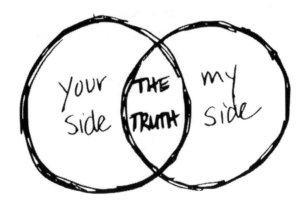

The actual truth, in the middle of the diagram, is objective and doesn't involve emotions. If one party is very emotional about what happened, I'm not invalidating it, but I'd rather just bring it back to the facts, which gives a different perspective. Nine times out of ten, when a child comes to you with a complaint or recounting of a story of what happened, there was something before and something after that occurred that has the potential to change your perspective about everything. Yes, everything.

More than once a child has come up to me and said, "Sally hit me with the rope." Sally is a cross-generational troublemaker. Before I jump out of my seat, I ask "Where was she and where were you? Oh, you were walking by and she was on the rope, swinging? Oh, so was she swinging before you got there? Yes, she was. Ah okay, well, when someone is swinging on the rope or getting ready to, they definitely need to make sure the path is clear, but also, no one should be walking in that area. Once someone starts swinging, they can't control the rope, so I don't think Sally hit you with the rope on purpose. I think you did get hit by the rope. What can everyone do differently so that this doesn't happen again?"

They might say, "Well, I can pay attention near the rope and Sally can yell for people to get out of the way." Then I would say, "Yes, that's a great idea!" Next, I would call Sally over to explain what happened. I wouldn't expect Sally to apologize, because frankly, she did nothing wrong and I'm not going to ask her to be responsible for the other child's emotions. I would say, "Hey this happened, it wasn't your fault, but if you ever see anyone, it's a good idea to yell 'Heads up!'" You can unpack the importance of this exchange by getting all the kids involved. At the very least, we are creating community amongst them.

We also have the coaches report little things to parents, especially when a child is upset, to get clear on the narrative. There's nothing like a 5-year-old kid going home and telling the story from their emotions rather than the facts. The truth can get lost. I want parents to understand that we have things handled, it was discussed already between all involved parties, and maybe their child is still working through their emotions. This is an opportunity for them to support their child at home and bring clarity to the situation.

Please keep asking questions before you come at me or another caregiver with metaphorical guns a blazing. Be willing to communicate with your child's caregivers to figure out what's going on. Calling the police should be for instances where there is real abuse and assault. Where your child's safety is intentionally disregarded or grossly neglected. Every circumstance is different, so take a deep breath, ask questions and communicate with your child and their caregiver or school. Accidents happen, and that doesn't negate an injury, but it also doesn't mean your child was targeted, abused, assaulted or neglected. Things will happen on your watch and things will happen on someone else's. This does not mean that you or other adults do not love your child or have their best interest at heart. Please know also, that childcare providers, coaches, teachers, and other positions of authority that work with minors are mandated reporters in most states. This means if any of these people suspect any abuse, whether at home, or their place of business, they must report it to the police.

What I tell my next-in-command is to get on the phone. Emails and texts are not the right way to discuss issues of this kind because you can't see intention on the other person's face or hear it in their voice if all you have is text. If I thought my child was being bullied or assaulted you bet your sweet ass I'd be on the phone.

Communicating through email and text belabors and drags out issues. It also gives people inflated courage to say things that they can't take back. Trust me, I've been on the receiving end of harassing and disparaging communication, and when asked to get on a call, I was ignored. To me, that means you just want to yell at me, and I'm sorry, that's not going to happen. I respect you and take your child's safety and happiness very seriously, but I will not let you use communication related to a specific incident as a way to intimidate me into submission or disparage my company or my staff. If you don't feel it's necessary to have a phone call or face to face conversation, then you should reconsider how important you think this is. I would also say that program may just not be the right fit for your family.

The bottom line is that we are all in this together. Kids need to learn at a young age to take care of themselves. That doesn't mean they are in this alone, it just means that *they* are their *own* first line of defense. There is such power and strength in knowing you can take care of yourself. Give your kids that opportunity. Talk to them.

Over dinner, play the game "High Low". Usually I do this on vacation, but over the dinner table is great each night! Ask your child or children, "What was your high today and what was your low?" Then have a discussion. Not eating together? Prioritize family dinners or even breakfasts. A few times a week should be your minimum.

Create opportunities for your child to open up to you. They aren't always going to bring things up, especially the instances where they felt really hurt. You are their advocate, but remember you will do a better job of advocating for them when you have all the facts. Defend your child, but not blindly or at the expense of others.

CHAPTER 12

When Is the Right Time?

Now that we've talked about the *how*, it's time to discuss the *when*. It seems like there isn't a consensus about when kids should start or be doing certain things. I think each child is differ nt, so you have to think about what is right for your family. Do *not* let fear decide for you. What types of things are we talking about? Chores, independence, phones, getting a job, and technology in general to name a few.

Chores, as we discussed, can start at any time. They need to be age-appropriate and you need to have realistic expectations. So, start 'em early. Children as young as 2 years old can have chores: and children even younger can participate in your chores. They will mimic what you're doing and want to be a part of it. Sometimes the exercise is in learning the motions rather than perfecting the action. What I mean is that life is practice, so let them practice at a young age and focus on the steps, not the outcome.

Creating independence is the hardest part. Remember, your goal as a parent or caregiver is to have your child leave the nest and create a life they love. They need to be independent to do that. Slowly, kids should start being given a sense of independence and responsibility over their own time and efforts as early as 5 or 6 years old

Again, this depends on each individual child, but start small and go from there. Send them to the front desk of your apartment building to pick up a package. Have them walk to the corner mailbox. Let them walk the few blocks to school, even if you stand there and watch for a bit. As a child gets more comfortable doing things solo, you can give them more independence.

We used to allow 5th graders in our after-school program. Now, we end at 4th grade. By the time a child is in 5th grade, even though it's still elementary school, they are old enough to go home after school and manage themselves for the few hours you are still at work.

In fact, it will be nice for them to have some alone time to decompress, do their own thing and manage their life. It's okay to give them some structure for those few hours. And letting them be home after school with no adult doesn't mean you have to let them entertain the neighborhood. Create boundaries and stick to them. That means if your child breaks the rules, there will be repercussions. A temporary hold of privileges or a full-on termination of privileges will work if warranted. Even for our coaches, I give them two chances. Once is a mistake, but twice is a habit. Find your own boundaries, clearly communicate them, and go from there.

What About Technology-Focused Independence?

Oh, technology and the never-ending debate about when it's appropriate. Screens do have their place. Like when toddlers need to be entertained at family dinners in a restaurant. Or when kids are sick or under the weather or mom, dad, or the caregiver just need a break. Technology is not a pacifier though, so create limits and share them with your child. Screens are tablets, TV, their adult's phone, and the like. Even if it's educational, you still need to limit things.

What about phones or watches for tweens and teens? Yes, there is a draw to giving them phones for safety reasons—I get that. But I personally don't think a child under the age of 11 needs a phone or watch. It might be a good idea for kids that are independent and on their own, but with limitations. I advise that they have something without download capabilities. For watches, they should be set up so that your child can only call you, the parent or caregiver. For phones, settings should be created to put on an automatic time-out for connectivity during hours when the phone would be a distraction, like when they are in school.

We've had kids as young as seven with an Apple watch and phone at camp. My first reaction was to ask myself, "Why?" First, there needs to be trust between parents and our sta and also our athletes and sta , and even between kids and parents. When you give your child unlimited access to you during the day, they often won't feel the need to invest in other relationships or sometimes even respect other adults. Second, don't you want to be o duty? You entrusted someone else with the care of your child. Let them do their job and you can enjoy your time apart.

In general, I don't see a need for tracking devices, but if your kid having one makes you feel better, great. We allow them at our camps, but with limitations. There can be no usage: it's to stay in the backpack. Plus, we are not responsible for lost, stolen, or damaged equipment. It is important for you to always lay out the rules and boundaries with your child when introducing technology. They shouldn't be glued to their phones when walking down the street. They need to stay present and aware of their surroundings and environment at the very least for safety's sake. Lean on the side of restriction versus free reign. It will save you lots of headaches in the long run.

Technology and screens create real addictions and impact our mental health more than we care to admit. Build a respect for them early on in your child's life: respect for their own health and wellness that is. At a recent tween/teen camp that yours truly ran, I asked the kids how many of them had phones. To my surprise most did not. I had one kid go on to say that he did have a phone and gave it back to his parents. His reason? "I was wasting too much time and I didn't like how I felt." Brave soul. So often kids will force themselves to fit in a box that doesn't fit. Take this advice for your own tech practices. See how your life improves without the tether or that phone or tablet!

What About Work?

Ah, here we see another age-old question: When should a child get a job? Well, they already have them in the house and they are called chores. Sometime during elementary school, when they start asking for big ticket items, it's time to have the money conversation and give them options for how they can earn some money doing additional chores. Remember, they don't get paid for their regular chores as it's their contribution to the family.

Check your town's rules on working papers and what jobs a minor can have. I have been working since I was 10 years old. My friend Becky and I shared a paper route and became blood sisters doing so—that's another story. Then I babysat. You read earlier about how the family I used to work for is one I'm still connected with and that they are now having their own babies. Yeah, that started when I was 11.

I had two jobs the semester I took off from college, in addition to babysitting of course. Teens *should* have jobs. It teaches them how to take and process feedback in a professional environment, how to be a part of a team, how to be responsible, and how to have a good work ethic. Also, well, it shows them what happens when they don't meet expectations, and, on the flip side, what can result from them exceeding expectations. And all from a source that isn't you. Sometimes it is good for us to hear and learn from someone that isn't a part of our family. I never believed my parents' accolades. I was much more receptive when I got recognition outside the home, because those people "didn't have to" say those things because they weren't my parents.

Teach them how to apply for jobs, what they need to do, and then work on financial literacy with their first paycheck. My job as the owner of the gym is to mentor our coaches so that when they leave (because they will if I've done a good job) they take a skill with them. That skill transfers to any job, regardless of whether it involves kids.

I want my coaches to know how to communicate with people who have authority, to show graciousness when given a bonus or gift from a client, and to be able to have hard conversations with other staff members and kids. Whatever skill you name, I want them leaving with some life skills beyond just how to play dodgeball. And yes, we play dodgeball.

By high school, kids should have a part time job in the summer at the very least, but hopefully all year. Encourage and support them, but don't do things for them. When parents approach me about hiring their kids I say "Yes, tell them to get in touch with me." If they don't, I won't go chasing them. The interested teens have to show some effort and interest. I don't need someone on the payroll who isn't interested in doing the job.

Lead With Logic

Choosing the right timing for these different events can be a challenge, but you do and will know in your heart what is appropriate. Lead with logic, acknowledge your fears, and choose based on what is going to further your child instead of making choices based on what will assuage your concerns. Consider also that what makes them more independent makes you more independent as well. Check in with your kids, too. Support their concerns or fears and tell them in their love language that you believe in them to take on the next challenge. It's a family affair after all.

CHAPTER 13

A Note on Parenting

Parenting, whether it's as the parent, an auntie, an uncle, or other caregiver, is hard. But, when you're the parent it can be even harder because they go home with you. Maybe that sounds like a joke, but I'm serious. It's so much easier for me to put my foot down and resist the temptation of giving in to repeated requests because I know my time with each kid is limited. That is also what inspires me to do better, I only have so much time with them. But when you are their person, you *are* their person—the one that your child feels most safe and comfortable with. And that means you get to see all the emotions and every side of that child.

With each joy, there will be a trying time. But you've got this. You cared enough about doing this right to read an entire book about how not to ruin your kid, and that's saying something. So, stay the course and make decisions that will benefit you and your child in the long term, not the right now. Sometimes it will take all of you and sometimes you'll still fail *and that is okay*. There is nothing wrong with failing. We are all just living life and practicing for what's next.

Even though your child may not be a baby anymore, you are always a first-time parent. Even my friends, whose children are 20 and 18, are first-time parents. They are parenting those individual 20- and 18-year-olds at that age for the first time. Each child is unique, and although past practice has a great impact, what is relatable to one child may not be to another. So, show yourself some grace. And your kids too. After all, it's the first time they are 6, 7, or 8 years old right now. They are figuring things out and stepping into life.

They need your guidance, rules, empathy, and, of course, love. Life is an adventure and sometimes you are dangling from the zipline. Other times you are firmly rooted on the ground. Try out both. Conflict and the land of uncomfortable are the places where the most growth and magic happens: so allow both yourself and your kids to work through those moments to come out the other side with more growth than you could have imagined!

Turn To Your Village

Remember, you aren't expected to go on the journey of raising kids alone. We don't live in multigenerational houses anymore if any of us even live near family at all. So, we need to create our communities out of our local neighborhoods and nearby parent groups that we can trust to parent our kids when we just cannot. Because there will be those days.

And then, you too can provide that network with the same support and step in when they need the help. Meet your neighbors, know your shopkeepers, say hello to the mailperson, take a visit to your local fire station, make your child known in the community and have them know the community. They can speak directly to adults and build relationships. Creating a collective community means someone is always looking out for you and your family. It establishes connectedness and belonging for everyone, which means we are all vested and want to make a difference for one another.

The Most Important Question

When you are working through all that comes with helping your child grow into an adult, remember your "why." Yeah, that thing we talked about in the beginning. What is the "why" behind the way you choose to parent your child? Yes, for them to be happy and fulfilled, but also to be independent: so give them the tools. Keep your why at your heart's center when making decisions, especially the hard ones. Do what is best for your child even if it scares you a little bit (or it scares them). Work together to get past those natural anxieties.

Also, research your schools and after care programs to make sure they are aligned with your why. Share with your nannies, babysitters, family members, and anyone else who watches your child what your why is and help guide it. Consider it an enrollment conversation, though, not a dictation. And be kind, it's okay for kids to have crazy spoiled time with grandma and grandpa or their auntie— or even *you*. It's great if everyone is on the same page, though, so you can all work together to provide essential opportunities for the child or children in your life.

Now, we don't always have the luxury, financial means, or opportunities to pick and choose schools, after-care programs or the like. That's okay. Just make the concessions where you can. If your child needs to be in after school activities provided by the school, have a conversation with the program about adding more outdoor time or make it a point to walk home with your child to give them outside time. You can even give them outside time before school. Be creative and find solutions.

Do good and keep your head up. Parenting is hard, but it is also oh-so rewarding.

I'll leave you with this...

When it comes to parenting:
- Be present
- Be consistent
- Be committed to the long game
- Be kind to yourself, your child and others

Remember that every day brings another opportunity to practice and be better. You are doing a great job!

All my love,
Michele

Parenting Got You Puzzled?

Get Expert Guidance Today

Book Your Private Coaching Session with Michele!

I'm Luna, and my mom knows how to help you unleash your parenting potential!

Send an Email to Book Your Appointment to *michele@kelbercoaching.com* Today!

Acknowledgements

They say it takes a village and it sure does.

Foremost in this process Patti, my marketing guru, I'd be lost without you. Thank you for your grace, support, and magic touch in getting my words out to the world.

Ken, my business coach and one of the few people so committed to my success that he could see past the bullshit.

Brian, Danny, Lizzie & Carrie, You made me a "teen mom" and I wouldn't have it any other way. Grateful beyond words to still be in each other's lives.

Jay & Christina, for always wanting me to win and believing in my vision and providing the place to make it a reality!

Christof & Johanna, I love you so much and am so thankful to be your Auntie. My heart is so full. You have taught me so much.

Judy, Real talk is underrated and so is a friend's eye on newly written pages.

Deanna, You are the apple of my eye and the only person I would trust to fulfill my dreams.

Gerry & Colette, Thank you for making me a parent and yet still treating me like a daughter and sister. It's our chosen family that often is our beacon.

Mom & Dad, Thank you for being revolutionaries and doing your best as parents even when life threw you curveballs. I think I did you proud.

Karl, This process and new chapter in my life wouldn't be possible without you. I see all that you have done and thank you from the bottom of my heart.

And lastly to all the families, kids, and coaches that have stepped through the doors of Gantry Kids & Teens. You have filled my life with joy, given me a few gray hairs, but most of all beat life into my heart over all these years. Thank you.

About the Author

Michele lives in Colorado, but will always have an East Coast attitude and love for NYC. She earned a BA in Art, with a Spanish Minor, then a JD and MBA. Michele is an accomplished human, having had careers in all those areas and now writing a lifelong goal. Her passion though is human connection and building relationships. She is committed to the growth and development of children as well as their parents and caregivers. Michele's goal is to enable children to know and use their voice in the world, contribute no matter their age, and be independent in what has become a somewhat daunting world. She puts a high priority on play both for children and herself! It is where the magic happens after all. Michele's love language is quality time and she spends much of it with her friends and family building lasting memories, traveling, and hiking with her 14-year-old dog Luna!

Made in the USA
Monee, IL
07 February 2024

ea5fb7fe-8541-4e3e-9b00-1a540774c566R01